RAILWAY
ARCHAEOLOGY

RAILWAY
ARCHAEOLOGY

O.S. Nock

Book Club Associates, London

Title pages *Killingworth Colliery locomotive. See page 27* (Crown Copyright).

This edition published 1981 by Book Club Associates, by arrangement with Patrick Stephens Limited.

Text photoset in 10 on 11 pt English Times by Manuset Limited, Baldock, Herts. Printed in Great Britain on 100 gsm Fineblade coated cartridge, and bound, by The Garden City Press, Letchworth, Herts.

Contents

A pictorial map, around 1900, showing the London and North Western Railway providing services all over Great Britain and much of Ireland! See page 35 (British Railways).

Introduction

Archaeology is defined as 'the science which deduces a knowledge of past times from the study of their existing remains'. In applying such a study to railways, as with any other crafts and cultures, there has to be a clear definition of parameters, and in this book, starting from the inception of steam traction, I have drawn the later boundary line at August 1914—not that I intend to concern myself only with locomotives: far from it. In approaching railway archaeology in its strictest sense one realises at once the extent to which true archaeology has become almost inextricably entwined with the more single-minded purpose of preserving and running steam locomotives, usually very much out of context with their true historical aspects. It is not surprising. In the age-old history of man on this planet there has surely been no single product of his inventiveness that has appealed more to the emotions; and so, when its regular commercial use came to an end and it was threatened with extinction, it was natural that from men and women of every estate there came an upsurge of effort in many dissimilar ways to preserve and restore favourite designs to working condition.

By the very nature of its attraction the steam locomotive became the centre-piece of interest on railways all over the world. In the 19th century in Great Britain the loving care lavished on its painting styles, and the discipline imposed upon those who had to clean it, were in vivid contrast to the dull humdrum appearance of the carriages, even of those in which first class passengers rode. Yet the close-coupled, bare-boarded four-wheelers that brought the 'workmen' of London in their tens of thousands into Liverpool Street or Ludgate Hill would be just as much a part of the railway archaeological scene as the immaculate locomotive that took 'The Flying Dutchman' out of Paddington. In the event, however, neither have survived. The trouble is railway relics are rather large, and need a great deal of space and continued maintenance for their successful preservation, and it is inevitable that what originates as a scientific study eventuates as an exercise in practical politics and the most ruthlessly hard economics. There was nothing more characteristic of railways in the 19th century than the English country station. Many of them were quite beautiful architectural period pieces, but the majority have now fallen into disuse. For a two-fold reason they have not been left *in situ*: clearing the site made for a slight reduction in rateable value of the land; the materials were usually so good, as to be readily saleable for a good price. There was a fine example of a Brunellian country station near my home which has disappeared for these very reasons.

In the absence of much in the way of tangible relics, in their original and natural environment, anyone seeking to build up an authentic picture of what railways were really like in the period from 70 to 150 years ago must necessarily begin in libraries rather than by excavations on site. There is, however, one place in Great Britain where a skilfully organised 'dig' might yield some fascinating results, but this is an exception, quite without parallel. Nevertheless, browsing in libraries and museums should be no more than the preliminary guide to the more interesting field work. The literature of railways is certainly immense, though a high proportion of it does not get down to the bedrock fundamentals which are essential to investigations in the archaeological sense. A great number of original drawings and plans have fortunately been preserved, and are available for serious study; but even these reveal no more than some of the hardware of the early railway age and, a little regrettably perhaps, some authors with the gift of writing vivid prose have drawn more on their own imagination than upon definite contemporary documentation. They have produced some delightful reading, but not quite the stuff of which true railway archaeology is to be made.

So how does one start? And how, when the limitations of the material available become revealed, does one restrict the field of study to something that can be covered thoroughly? It is very much a case of individual choice. Many enthusiasts have studied locomotive families and dynasties in depth; others have written entertainingly about carriages, and wagons, but few attempts have been made to bring the whole scene together. Strangely enough some of the most complete pictures of the railway scene can be seen from the voluminous reports made by Inspecting Officers of the Board of Trade after their enquiries into the cause of accidents. These often give a clear insight into the work of enginemen, train crews, signalmen, station staff, passengers, and even top management.

I was very interested and impressed by a visit I made a few years ago to the Old Sacramento State Historic Park, California, which includes a most skilfully researched railway exhibit. There are not only two beautifully restored 'period' locomotives, but they, and the passenger cars to which they are attached, stand in a period station, or depot as they call them in America; and the entire paraphernalia of travel is there to be seen, including luggage, tickets, advertising bills, and figures in waxwork representing enginemen, and the agent in the booking office. In York one can see in the Castle Museum how magnificently the same theme can be applied to an English street scene. In this book I have had the temerity to suggest where one or two railway tableaux might be developed.

In looking back over the vast field in which I have ventured to tread in this book I am conscious of the immense debt of gratitude which I owe to countless people, over practically my whole life. To mention even a few of them, and their various associations with parts of the story, would add at least another chapter. At this distance in time, few of them, if they were still alive, would be in the least bit conscious of how they *had* helped. In my family circle I am credited with something of a photographic memory—except for domestic matters!—and in putting this particular story together many experiences and expeditions of my childhood have come to mind; and those, together with recent ones of a more professional nature, make up a kaleidoscope of memories for which I can only express a big and highly diversified thank you to everyone concerned.

O.S. Nock, Batheaston, Bath
August 1980

Chapter 1

The elements
I—Formation, track and vehicles

Rather more than 40 years ago that great scholar of the world of transportation history, Charles E. Lee, startled the Permanent Way Institution by tracing the origin of railways back to Babylonian times—more than 2000 BC. It was a masterly exposition, such as might have been expected by those of us who knew him; and, of course, he was taking the word 'railways' in its most literal sense, as that of any activity which ran on rails. In the archaeological sense I am, by comparison, concerned with modern, almost contemporary history for, although in the introduction to this book I did set the earlier parameter at the beginning of steam traction, if one is to co-ordinate the process of evolution in Great Britain to its logical beginnings, it must be tied into the Industrial Revolution, and that was in full blast long before the end of the 18th century. So the pages of history must be turned back to the early days of the Hanoverian dynasty in what was then, in little more than name, the 'United Kingdom'.

In what might be called the 'run-up' to the Industrial Revolution the conveyance of passengers by railway was about the last thing that even the most advanced pioneers contemplated. The earliest activity was concerned almost entirely with minerals, and that led to works in some unexpected and inhospitable areas. The English scene of 250 to 300 years ago would have given little suggestion of the transformation that followed, at a time when the Government of the day was more concerned with dealing with the second Jacobite rebellion than with what Thomas Newcomen was doing down in Cornwall, or with mining developments in County Durham.

It can be recalled, perhaps with some surprise, that James Watt and Bonnie Prince Charlie were contemporaries, and that one of the most picturesque railways in the north was already in operation when the Highland army marched south from Edinburgh, occupied Carlisle and then 'invaded' England, by way of Shap Fell and Lancaster, in 1745. Although the situation was naturally tense, the eastern side of the country was unmolested by that audacious march of the clans. In the far west the significance of what was stirring in the mining districts of Cornwall was as yet unrelated to transport, and the story of railway origins, in their physical relics and in their documentation, belongs in the main to County Durham. It is a picturesque and fascinating starting point.

One is, at the same time, confronted by two aspects of such a study: firstly, the basic hardware of rails and the vehicles that ran upon them and secondly, the underlying formation on which the rails were laid. The fundamental object of using rails, apart from guiding vehicles on a 'straight and narrow' path, was to enable heavier loads to be conveyed; and, when some of the most important of the early coal mining activities in County Durham became established in the wild country on the eastern slopes of the Pennines, it was not merely a case of laying down some form of railway. The high ridges and deep clefts of that rough countryside had to be traversed if the coal was to be conveyed to the sea or to a navigable river. So, at the very dawn of the modern age of transportation by rail, three of the elements most vitally concerned in its development were closely linked, in West Durham: the road-bed, its alignment and grading; the rails themselves, and the wagons in which the mineral was conveyed. There was, nevertheless, a fourth element inherent in the business, which was at first no more than indirectly linked to activities in Durham—that of motive power.

It does not need much study of a large-scale contoured map of Upper Weardale to appreciate something of the extremely hilly terrain. It was little less so, east of the Derwent, and the opening of a great coalfield at Tanfield, roughly a mile north-west of Stanley, led to the construction in the 1720s of the longest and most remarkable wagon-way that had so far been enterprised. An eminent antiquary of that time, Dr William Stukeley, had been making a detailed examination of the Roman Wall in 1725, and coming afterwards to Newcastle and hearing of the wagon-way under construction, he turned aside to see it. With the eye and sensitivity of the historian he appreciated that here was a work every bit as significant in perspective as the Roman Wall itself, and he wrote enthusiastically of his visit, where others might have deplored the spoilation of the countryside. Some of the engineering features were indeed astonishing in their magnitude alone, quite apart from the duty they were originally called upon to perform. Imagine, for example, constructing an embankment 100 feet high and 300 feet wide at the base in order to provide a good alignment and easy gradients for a line of railway designed, in the first place, for nothing more onerous than horse-drawn coal wagons.

The Tanfield Embankment, the oldest in the world built for the express purpose of carrying a railway, is a monument of outstanding archaeological importance, though today it would be a case of cutting, rather than the traditional digging that would be needed to reveal its imposing bulk into full view, because the trees have grown so thickly on its banks, sweeping down to the Beamish Burn, as to make it all but invisible. Then nearby is the even more amazing Causey Arch. This structure was made possible by George Bowes joining the business partnership which became known as 'The Grand Allies', and he contributed his share towards the building of the five-mile long wagon-way from Tanfield to the River Tyne by financing the construction of the great viaduct over the Beamish Burn. But for this, great inconvenience and delay would have been involved in carrying the line across this deep glen, even as was necessary on the Stanhope and Tyne Railway, (to be mentioned later) in negotiating Hownes Gill.

At the time it was built, in 1725, the Causey Arch as a structure was nothing very much out of the ordinary. Its supreme importance, like the Tanfield Embankment, lay in its use, exclusively, for a railway. It is a slightly flattened arch of 102 feet span, in freestone. It rises 35 feet above the points of springing of the arch, and it was made wide enough to carry two tracks of 4 feet gauge abreast of each other. When originally built to the designs of Ralph Wood, a local master mason, its appearance, spanning the glen, was certainly spectacular, as can be judged from the drawing by Thomas Jameson reproduced

The Causey Arch from a drawing by Thomas Jameson made at the time of the construction (Tomlinson's North Eastern Railway).

in the classic book—*Tomlinson's North Eastern Railway, 1914;* but like the embankment, the subsequent afforestation of the glen has so encompassed the arch making it all but invisible. There is, however, in this area, scope for a tremendous reconstruction of what an 18th century wagon-way was like. The formula has certainly been displayed in the open air museum at Beamish. The Tanfield line, which in due course became a mineral branch of the North Eastern Railway, was complete in all its constructional aspects, having deep cuttings as well as high embankments. The only thing it did not include was a tunnel of any length.

Before long the line was being very heavily used. It is recorded that, in 1732, an average of 400 wagons of the Newcastle chaldron type were passing over it every day, each having a weight of 53 hundredweight. For a detailed description of the track that was carrying such a traffic we are indebted to a French observer, M Gabriel Jars. When the formation had been prepared and suitably

A relatively recent photograph of the Causey Arch.

graded the cross timbers were laid at a pitch that seemed to vary between two and three feet. The rails themselves, also of wood, were six to seven inches wide by five inches deep, spaced to provide a rail gauge of four foot. They were fastened to the cross timbers by wooden pegs. Although the wagon-ways of ancient times consisted of carefully aligned stone blocks to guide wheels having no flanges, the wagon-ways in the north-east, in using wooden rails to guide flanged wheels, had to import timber of the requisite quality. At that time England relied upon the finest oak from the New Forest or Sussex for her giant sailing battleships, and it was from the same sources that oak for the railways of the north-east was also obtained, shipped to Sunderland or Newcastle.

More than 250 years have elapsed since the opening of what has been claimed as the oldest railway in the world; but a courageous activity in the area began in 1970 when the National Coal Board closed its steam shed at Marley Hill, near the point where its Bowes Railway crossed the route of the Tanfield Line. The Stephenson & Hawthorns Locomotive Trust was formed to acquire a representative collection of those built in the Tyneside area, and Marley Hill shed became a centre of locomotive preservation in the north-east. Nevertheless, preservation of locomotives is only one step towards a desire to run them, and where better than over such historic ground as that of the Tanfield Railway? How permission was eventually obtained to lay track over half a mile of former British Railways land from Marley Hill northward to Bowes Bridge was an epic in itself, and it is not difficult to sense and share in the elation felt by those responsible when, on Jubilee weekend, in 1977, passenger trains ran once again, and the 'Oldest Railway in the World' was back in business.

Of course, it was very far from 'preservation' in its truest sense, and one looks wistfully southwards from that junction point where the short connecting curve to Marley Hill engine shed joins the 'main line', because less than a mile beyond that junction is the Causey Arch. Could there not some day be a true,

Very early railways in County Durham.

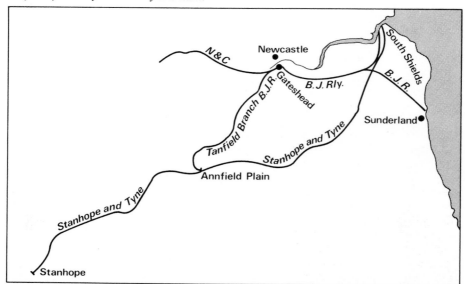

fully authoritative reconstruction of what a wagon-way was like 250 years ago? A train of chaldron wagons should not be unduly expensive to construct and such an enterprise, to give rides to fare-paying passengers, would have the priceless advantage that the four-legged motive power would be no more than part time! I am sure that such a reconstruction could prove a tourist attraction of the greatest value, because there the complete scene of pioneer transportation on rails could be presented. The Tanfield embankment and the Causey Arch by themselves convey little to the imagination; but lay down a track of wooden rails, and run a shuttle 'service' of chaldron wagons trundled along by horses over these 'lions' of railway history, and one would have a living exhibit of outstanding importance—including a driver in correct period costume.

There are not many places remaining today where such an unrivalled opportunity exists as on the Tanfield line. Not far away, to the south-west, is Hownes Gill. This is a dry ravine, 160 feet deep but no less than 800 feet wide and, when the Stanhope and Tyne Railway was first projected in the early 1830s, it was proposed to build a viaduct. But it would have been a very costly undertaking for what was no more than another colliery wagon-way and, at what is believed to be a suggestion of Robert Stephenson, an extraordinary system of operation was devised, and worked for many years until the stately 12-arch viaduct was completed in 1858. This latter stands today, but the machinery by which wagons were originally lowered down one side of the ravine, and hauled up the other, can only be conjectured from early drawings and contemporary descriptions. If any model steam enthusiast could be lured away from locomotives to attempt a working reconstruction of Hownes Gill, in '0' gauge ($\frac{1}{4}$ inch to the foot) with appropriate scenic embellishments, he would create an archaeological period piece of the first importance.

The winding engine was at the foot of the ravine, but the slopes were so steep—1 in $2\frac{1}{2}$ on one side and 1 in 3 on the other—that the wagons could not be taken down and up on a continuation of the ordinary tracks. There were special cradle trucks, with unequal sized wheels in which the railway wagons were carried athwartships, being turned at right angles to their normal direction on turntables at the top of each steep incline. Only one wagon was conveyed at a time, and by moving one loaded and one empty simultaneously, one down and one up, the power required from the winding engine was reduced to that of the paying load. On each side of the ravine the ordinary tracks approached on more gradual inclines. The loaded wagons from the west and the returning empties arrived at the respective brinks by gravity, with the horses riding in dandy carts behind—another picturesque touch for a model of the activity. Hownes Gill certainly provides a tantalisingly classic example of the situation that frequently confronts those who would delve into the archaeology of railways, and find themselves dependent almost entirely upon drawings and contemporary descriptions, rather than actual physical remains.

The situation is better with the track itself; and its development from the simple, though robust, type of the period 1725 to 1775 is documented in many contemporary illustrations, and by actual examples in the National Railway Museum and elsewhere. To gather a more complete picture of operation on Tanfield wagon-way, and also on other lines serving the collieries in the Tyne and Wear area, the typical Newcastle chaldron wagon of the day must be described. Most of these early wagon-ways were designed for gravity operation, the loaded direction of running being generally downhill from the higher

A plan of the gravity worked inclines at Hownes Gill (Tomlinson's North Eastern Railway).

ground, beneath which were found so many of the richest coal seams, to river level; and it was characteristic of these wagon-ways to build the wagons with different sized wheels front and back, so as to keep the load approximately level on the downhill run. The leading pair of wheels, which was the larger, were often of iron with spokes, while the rearward pair were of solid wood, often of birch.

Although it was found that horses could pull several of these heavy wagons on an easily graded route or on the level, it appears to have been usual to have one horse to a wagon. The driver rode on the wagon most of the time and, when coasting down grade, he would be throwing all his weight on to the brake lever, which acted upon the rearward wooden wheels. The horse meanwhile would be trotting along behind. As the Industrial Revolution gathered momentum in the north-east and more wagon-ways were built, the timber suppliers in the south began to cash in on the situation, and materials were shipped to the Tyne and Wear regardless of whether they had been ordered or not. Rails in beech and ash, as well as oak, were indiscriminately dumped, until the dealers in Sunderland had six to nine months stock on hand. The best quality oak rails sold at about 6d (2½p) per yard! Nicholas Wood (the celebrated mining engineer, and one of the judges at the Rainhill locomotive trials in 1829) in his *Treatise on Railways* stated that, in 1738, cast iron was first used as a *substitute* for oak in rails; but then he added the somewhat extraordinary statement that '. . . owing to the old wagons continuing to be employed, which were of too much weight for the cast iron, they did not completely succeed in the first attempt'. What those very early cast iron rails were like was not disclosed!

The first successful use of iron as a material for rails was made on the wagon-way constructed on the river Severn to the Coalbrookdale Ironworks in 1750, and afterwards extended to Ketley a total distance of five miles. This wagon-way was built to convey coal ferried up the river to the smelting furnaces at Horsehay and Ketley, and was originally laid with track on the style of the Durham lines. By the year 1767, however, the demand for pig iron fell to a very low level. To have cut down production in the extensive smelting plants would have been uneconomic as well as very costly when it came to stepping up production once more, and so a novel way of stocking the 'pigs' was devised which, at the same time, would benefit the maintenance of the wagon-way. They decided to make them in such a form that they could be laid on the top of the rails—5 feet long, 4 inches wide, and 1½ inches thick, with three holes to make the necessary fastening. By this means they had a very convenient and advantageous way of stocking them, and equally a means of lessening the wear on the rails themselves. The procedure had the great advantage that, if there was a sudden increase in the demand for pig iron, the rail-tops could be taken up and sold. As a first experiment between five and six tons of 'rails' were cast in November 1767; but it proved so successful that in the years 1768 and 1771 no less than 800 tons of cast iron rail-tops were produced, and what had begun as a temporary expedient became a permanent feature, for a time at any rate.

Up to this time the wagon-ways that had been built had all been for the exclusive use of the owners of one or another of the great industrial enterprises; but their very success led to another important phase of railway evolution which came to have a marked effect upon the basic hardware. With the Industrial Revolution there was developing an extensive network of canals. These were not intended as private concerns, solely for the use of their owners, but as public toll highways available to anyone who had a boat and could pay the toll. In time, also, a system of light railways was developed, to feed the canals. Before coming to the equipment of these railways there was an event, in Sheffield, that had a widespread influence. The Duke of Norfolk owned some collieries on the outskirts of the town and, to facilitate transport of the coal to a central depot, he built a wagon-way in the traditional style, with wooden rails over a distance of about two miles. The local people were not amused. It was thought that its object was to increase the price of coal, by refusing to sell at the pit head. Hitherto purchasers had been allowed to use their own transport to take it away. Feeling ran high enough to develop into a riot, in which the rails and many of the wagons were destroyed by fire. That was in 1774, but out of it there arose a new conception, of having public railways on which the vehicles both of the owners and of the public could be accommodated and which would, at the same time, provide the guidance and smooth riding of one of the older wagon-ways.

Although the plate rail that developed from this situation, of angle section, with the upturned edge on the inside, proved to be no more than a passing phase in the evolution of railways as we know them today, it did postulate a principle that has had examples in much more recent times, and is indeed

An example of a plate-way with flanges on the inside: Little Eaton, near Derby (Crown Copyright).

Trains of chaldron type wagons, drawn by a team of horses, on the Little Eaton plate-way (Crown Copyright).

practised on a limited scale in the USA today—that of having vehicles which can be used at will either on a road, or on a railway. The vehicles that ran on the plate-ways of 200 years ago had wheels with flangeless tyres. The angled shape of the plates provided the guides to keep the vehicles correctly positioned on the plates while, of course, the hard and relatively smooth surface greatly reduced the rolling resistance and enabled horses to pull heavier loads than they could on the very poor highways of that era. But, of course, there was great operational convenience in being able to pull the wagons on to a road surface, however bad, if they were required to go beyond the extent of the plate-ways.

It is with this passing phase that the name of Benjamin Outram is most prominently associated, so much so that the term tram-road, or tram-way has actually been considered as derived from the engineer's name. This is not so. In his monumental paper to the Permanent Way Institution, Charles E. Lee traced the origin of the name tram in England, back to the reign of King James I, and meaning then a beam of wood. Thus the term tram-way in its true sense could be taken as meaning a log road. But, although the association of the name with that of Outram is quite fallacious, he was enthusiastic enough in promoting the development of the angled plate ways. He had every reason to be, as one of the partners in the Butterley Ironworks, established in 1792. One of his most important contributions to the main development of railways, however, was not in the rails, or plates, themselves but in the foundations. Not for him the cross timber, used in the north-east, and then at Coalbrookdale. He recommended '. . . the Rail-way to be made substantial, upon my improved plan, with stone blocks for the rails to rest upon: the rails to be of the stoutest cast iron, one yard in length, and to weigh about 37 lb. each . . .'. He reckoned that on such a track one horse would be able to haul a paying load of 10 to 12 tons of coal.

It was, however, one of Outram's partners in the Butterley Company, William Jessop, who can be set down as the true founder of modern railway permanent way. It was, of course, in the interest of his company that rails should be made in iron rather than wood; but there was no small difficulty in getting accurately shaped lengths of the requisite qualities of hard timber. It would seem that increasing demand had led to deterioration in the finish, from many suppliers. Be that as it may, Jessop designed—and in 1789 patented—a cast iron rail, the proportions of which were carefully suited to the distribution of stresses caused by a load rolling along it. In these days one reads a good deal about computer-aided engineering design, but a study of Jessop's rail of 1789 shows a masterly appreciation of all the factors involved. He, like his colleague, Outram, advocated supporting the rails on stone blocks, and his cast iron rails were of approximately the same length, namely three feet.

By casting his rails, Jessop was able to design them providing materials in relation to the distribution of stresses. Thus, seen broadside-on, the shape was fish-bellied, with a greater depth of web at the centre. The web was quite thin in proportion to the head of the rail, where greater width was needed to provide a wearing surface. At the ends the bottom flange was splayed out to make a steady support on the stone block and, seen end-on, was clearly a precise prototype of the type of rail now standard on British Railways. The early records indicate that, although the patent is dated 1789, the first rails of this kind were cast one year earlier, and were laid on a railway near Loughborough. While noting the change from timber to stone supports for the rails advocated by Outram and Jessop, a suggested origin of the name 'sleeper' for the cross timbers is referred to in Lee's paper. As distinct from the longitudinal timbers, or rails, which carried the rolling, or 'live' loads, the supporting cross-timbers were sometimes referred to as dormant, or sleeping—thus, the 'sleepers'.

Another interesting use of cast iron rails, in what could be regarded as a

An example of a plate-way with flanges on the outside, showing point work (Crown Copyright).

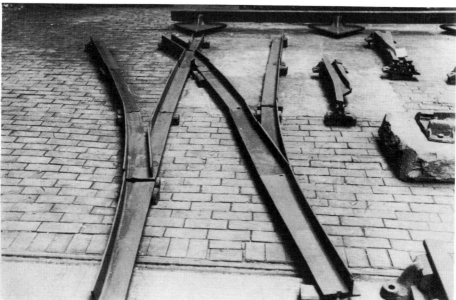

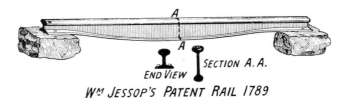

END VIEW   SECTION A.A.

Wᴹ JESSOP'S PATENT RAIL 1789

SECTION

LAWSON COLLIERY NEWCASTLE-ON-TYNE 1797

LOSH & STEPHENSON'S PATENT CAST RAIL 1816

Early forms of rail from The Railway Gazette, *June 11 1937.*

further prototype, was made in 1797 by Thomas Barnes, on a railway from Lawson Main Colliery, near Newcastle, to the river Tyne. Unlike Jessop, Barnes cast his rails to a uniform cross-section, without the fish-bellied feature, and had a separate support casting to secure them to the stone blocks. This use of a uniform section was a reversion to the timber longitudinal principle, except that Barnes' rail had a broad head, like Jessop's, to provide a good wearing surface. It was not only in his pioneer work with railways, but also in mining, that Barnes seemed to be one of the rising stars of the industrial development in the north-east; but, only four years after his introduction of iron rails on the Lawson Colliery line, at the early age of 36, he died. Historically, it was in his use of a uniform section of rail, and a 'chair' to support it at the ends, that Barnes' rail must be specially noted.

Chapter 2

The elements
II—Motive power

Having reached the last years of the 18th century it is now time to leave development of the track for a while to look at motive power. For its very beginnings we have to take our own enquiries back more than 100 years. It was prior to 1700 that a Frenchman, Dionysius Papin, produced one of the earliest examples of a piston working in a cylinder. Certain it is that in 1698, at Totnes, Devon, an inventor working entirely on an amateur basis, Thomas Savery, obtained a 21-year patent for a similar device and leased the manufacturing rights to Thomas Newcomen. From this entirely theoretical conception were evolved the first steam pumping engines used in the tin mines of Cornwall, though Newcomen, for all his mechanical skill, does not seem to have been a very imaginative operator. The story of how a great improvement in the working of these engines was made quite accidentally by one of the youths, who had the tedious job of sitting beside, and operating the cocks that regulated the upward and downward stroke of the pistons, makes good reading; and it leads on to the entry of James Watt and his partner, Matthew Boulton, to the developing scene.

Again, Watt's own first introduction to steam engines occurred almost by accident, when he was working as mathematical instrument maker at Glasgow University. During the 1763-4 session Professor John Anderson asked him to repair a model of a Newcomen engine which belonged to the Natural Philosophy Class in the college. It was a job after Watt's own heart, although he knew nothing about the engine before seeing the model. The actual work of repair was not difficult, but when it was in operation again he found that the boiler was not large enough to keep the model going for more than a few strokes. Continuous working would be impossible unless some economy in steam consumption could be made. The model worked just like the earliest Newcomen engines, with steam applied only during the upward stroke, and with a douche of cold water sprayed on to the outside of the cylinder to condense the steam inside and allow the piston to fall for the downward stroke. How Watt conceived the idea of having a separate condenser, during a meditative Sunday afternoon walk upon Glasgow Green, is one of the classics of industrial history; but, so far as railways were concerned, his subsequent success in the steam pumping engine business brought him into Cornwall, and into competition with the local interests.

One can sense the business acumen of Matthew Boulton in not being content with selling engines to the Cornish tin mines. He must have a resident engineer on the spot and so, 16 years after that memorable walk on Glasgow Green,

Boulton & Watt sent a young engineer named William Murdock to set up an office in Redruth. He soon came into contact with, and opposition to, that great Cornish engineer, Richard Trevithick; for while Murdock was busy installing Watt's engines, Trevithick was going all out to circumvent Watt's patents. The essential difference between the two was that Watt used low pressure steam, condensing it after use, while Trevithick was a high pressure man, exhausting the steam to atmosphere after each stroke with a puffing sound, that gained for his engines the nickname of 'puffers'. At the outset of his association with Boulton, James Watt had included the possible use of steam for land transport in his patents; but in the reticent nature of him nothing was developed, and it seems as though he discouraged his staff from pursuing things in that direction.

Murdock, away in Cornwall, had other ideas and surreptitiously began to work upon the idea of a self-propelled carriage. He made a model and tried it out one dark night on a walk leading to Redruth church. Accounts vary as to the encounters he had with local residents—one with the parson, who thought that the devil was after him! But, by the year 1786, his experiments reached the point when he felt confident to report back to the firm, in Birmingham. Their reaction was unfavourable and he was dissuaded from pursuing his ideas any further. Boulton afterwards wrote: '. . . I am persuaded I can cure him of the disorder or turn the evil to good!' Murdock, the most loyal of men, stifled his disappointment and, in 1799, was recalled from Cornwall to take up the important appointment of manager of Boulton & Watt's works in Birmingham. There is a model of his road carriage in the Birmingham Art Gallery. Had it not been for the very conservative attitude of the firm, Murdock, and the firm of Boulton & Watt, could have had the honour of producing the first steam locomotive.

So the way was left clear for Richard Trevithick. His home was within a few hundred yards of where Murdock lived when he was representing Boulton & Watt, in Redruth, and in a relatively small community he would undoubtedly have heard of the adventure on the church path! Whether he actually talked to Murdock, and learned of the firm's decision not to have anything to do with locomotives, we do not know, but it was 11 years after the official report to Birmingham of Murdock's model before Trevithick had a model of his own ready for trial. Whereas Boulton & Watt definitely clamped down on Murdock's activities, Trevithick had the support of influential friends, and the first trial of a high-pressure steam 'puffer' was made in the kitchen of his home, with Davies Gilbert, later to become President of the Royal Society, acting as fireman, and Lady De Dunstanville, wife of one of the largest landowners in Cornwall, as driver!

The point that stands out above all others in recalling most of Richard Trevithick's activities in locomotion, between the years 1798 and 1808, is that of the carefree, happy-go-lucky spirit in which epoch-marking advances in the technique of mechanical transport were approached. This was in some contrast to his keen perception of the fundamental points involved. For example, after the successful kitchen-table trial of his first model road locomotive he was concerned as to whether contact between the wheels and the road surface would provide sufficient adhesion to enable the locomotive to pull a load on the ordinary highway. So, in 1801, he and Davies Gilbert (Giddy, as his name then was) made the first ever experiment in measuring what we now call train resistance. They took a one-horse chaise and together pushed it up some of the

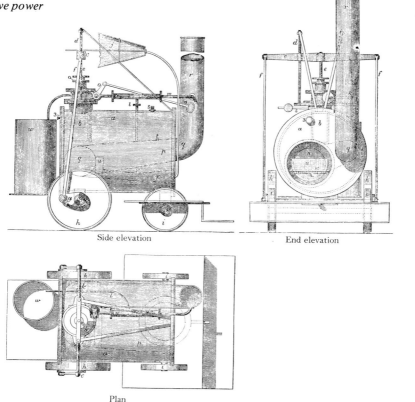

Side elevation   End elevation

Plan

Trevithick's 'road carriage', tested at Camborne, 1802, from a drawing by his third son, Francis, later locomotive superintendent, Northern Division, LNWR (Richard Trevithick, the engineer and the man).

hills of Camborne to judge the effort involved, and to make sure that the wheels did not skid through lack of adhesion.

The famous Camborne 'road carriage' was built in that same year and ran its first trial on Christmas Eve. What this vehicle was really like can never now be known with absolute certainty. His third son, Francis, biographer of his father, and Chief Mechanical Engineer of the Northern Division of the London and North Western Railway from 1847 to 1857, made a beautifully detailed drawing of it from the recollections of men who were involved, and not least from those of his father; but, according to contemporary accounts, the framing on which spectators were invited to jump for a ride, was made of wood. This suggestion is supported by the hilarious end to the second trial, which took place on December 28 1801. The first trial, on Christmas Eve, was made on Beacon Hill, Camborne, which had a gradient of 1 in 20. The carriage, however, had insufficient power to climb the hill, and stalled, from insufficient steam.

They tried again, four days later, intending to run from Camborne church to Tehidy House, where Lord De Dunstanville lived; they apparently started off in good style but, on coming to a gully having an open water course across the road, the steering handle was jerked out of the hand of Andrew Vivian, who was with Trevithick and doing the steering, and the carriage turned over. For

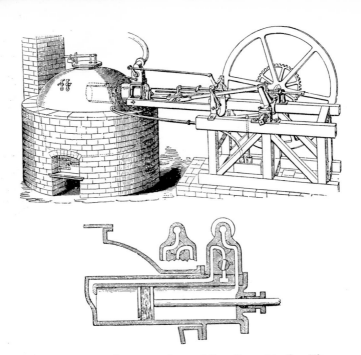

Trevithick's high pressure stationary engine and the adjacent boiler. The manner in which this cylinder extended into this boiler should be noted (Richard Trevithick, the engineer and the man).

the day, that was that; but Trevithick and Vivian were far from dismayed. They pushed the thing off the road and into the shelter of a nearby hotel. Forgetting apparently that there was still a fire in the road carriage they retired to the hotel, ordered a sumptuous meal of roast goose and 'proper drinks' and forgot all about locomotion until all the water in the carriage boiler had become evaporated, the metal red hot, and the wooden staging and everything else consumable—including the hotel shelter!—had gone up in flames. It was fortunate that they were then warned, because otherwise the hotel might have gone up as well.

Trevithick's experiments continued with carriages designed to run on the highway, and there was another exciting episode with the steering on a nocturnal run in London, when they ran into a garden wall, and tore down the railings. His preoccupation with road haulage led to the ever famous demonstration in South Wales in 1804, which, characteristic of so much of Trevithick's life, was the result of a wager between two ironmasters. There was then a plate-way from the Pen-y-Darran ironworks, near Dowlais, and about a mile north of Merthyr Tydfil, down the valley of the river Taff to the basin of the Glamorganshire Canal at Abercynon, then known as Navigation House. This was the route followed in later years by the main line of the Taff Vale Railway. By the year 1803 Trevithick's high pressure stationary engine was very much in demand for a diversity of purposes. So enthusiastic as to its potentialities was Samual Homfray of the Pen-y-Darran ironworks that he purchased a quarter part of Trevithick's patent on it, and flogged it for all it was worth in South Wales. He was a man of immense energy—astute in business, but also fond of cards and horse-racing; and, when Trevithick began to develop the engine towards locomotion on the plate-ways, he made a bet with Anthony

Hill, a fellow ironmaster, that he would haul ten tons of iron by steam locomotive from Pen-y-Darran down to Abercynon, a distance of 9¾ miles.

The audacious nature of the challenge was typical both of Homfray's sporting instincts and of Trevithick, who, needless to say, took up the project with immense gusto. To him adventures like this were of the very breath of life. No locomotive was then in existence. No one knew, with any certainty, how the plate-way would stand up to the weight of a machine large enough to haul those ten tons specified in the bet—and nobody seemed to care. That it was being done for a bet seemed to be the main thing and, when the locomotive arrived at Pen-y-Darran early in 1804, and the fire was first lit in it, public interest began to rise to fever heat, as with some great sporting contest like a horse race or a prize fight, rather than the overture to the beginning of an entirely new era in transport. Trevithick had, of course, put an immense amount of work into the design and construction of the locomotive, and from the outset it seems to have worked well. Writing to Davies Giddy—as he still was at that time—in February 1804, in a letter that revealed his spelling was not so good as his engineering skill, Trevithick said:

'The publick is much taken up with it. The bet of 500 Hundred Guineas will be desided abt the end of this week, and your pressence wod give mee moore satisfactn than you can consive, and I dought not but you will be satisfyde for the toil of the journey by a sight of the engine. The steam thats disscharged from the engine is turned up the chimney abt 3 feet above the fire, and when the engine is working 40 st pr mt, 4½ ft Stroake, Cylinder 8¼ In Diam, not the slightest particle of steam appears out of the top of the chimney, tho' the Chimney is but 8 feet above where the steam is delivered into it, neither is any steam at a distance nor the smallest particle of water to be found. I think its made a fix'd air from the heat of the Chimney. The fire burns much better when the steam goes up the chimney than what it do when the engine is idle . . .'.

Fortunately details of this ever famous 'Tram Locomotive', as it was called, are well documented. There is a fine elevation and end drawing of it in the Science Museum, at South Kensington, and the spirit of the great trial run, on

The celebrated 'tram engine' used in the famous trial run on the Pen-y-Darran plate-way in 1803 (Richard Trevithick, the engineer and the man).

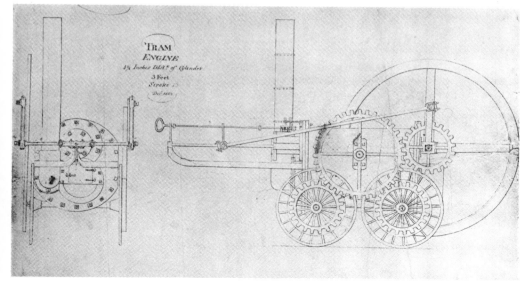

February 21 1804, has been magnificently captured in one of Terence Cuneo's superb paintings. So far as the actual run was concerned, it is astonishing that no preliminary check up on the route was made. One would have thought that Samuel Homfray, who was so vitally interested in the outcome, would have seen that there were no physical obstructions; but Trevithick himself records that they had to stop, to cut down some trees which were growing across the fairway, and elsewhere there were some large rocks that had to be moved out of the way. But the bet said nothing about speed, and the journey of $9\frac{3}{4}$ miles was eventually completed in 4 hours 5 minutes. Moreover, they carried not only the requisite ten tons of iron, in five wagons, but 70 men riding on those wagons. This would have increased the load by $3\frac{1}{2}$ to 4 tons. Having won the bet for Homfray, Trevithick went on to show that the locomotive could haul considerably heavier loads, but unhappily the situation between Homfray and his challenger, Anthony Hill, developed into a wrangle, with the latter raising every conceivable objection to paying up.

Cuneo painted another magnificent picture of the Pen-y-Darran locomotive, based, believe it or not, on a sketch made by no less a celebrity of later years than F.W. Webb, Chief Mechanical Engineer of the London and North Western Railway from 1871 to 1903. In 1857, only one year after he had completed his pupilage under Francis Trevithick, son of the mighty Richard, and then an assistant to him, Webb made an imaginative, allegorical drawing showing in clever juxtaposition master creations of the Trevithicks, father and son. Below, and in the foreground was the Pen-y-Darran engine, while on a bridge crossing the line at right angles was Francis Trevithick's 8 foot 6 inch single *Cornwall*. In Webb's sketch the latter engine is not shown in its original condition, with the boiler beneath the driving axle, but with a boiler of 1854, in which the centre-line of the boiler barrel, and that of the driving axle, coincided. Cuneo's painting shows the *Cornwall* in a still later form, as rebuilt at Crewe in 1858 with an orthodox boiler, but the Pen-y-Darran engine of Richard Trevithick is portrayed in its original form, running on a plate-way supported on stone blocks.

Above left *A painting by Terence Cuneo of the trial run of the Trevithick engine. Note Trevithick himself on the right, walking ahead with a spanner, to tighten up anything that came loose and (behind the dog) a man with a saw to cut down trees in the way!*

Above *A sketch, by F.W. Webb, in 1857, of an imaginary juxtaposition of famous engines by the Trevithicks, father and son: the Pen-y-Darran engine is at lower left; Francis Trevithick's 8 foot 6 inch 2-2-2* Cornwall *is on the bridge.* **Below** *Cuneo's painting of the same scene.*

So, by the first years of the 19th century the elements of railways had been created, albeit in a series of rather crude forms. But the world was ready for the astonishing evolution that followed. In the same year as the ever-famous run at Pen-y-Darran, Christopher Blackett, the owner of the Wylam Colliery in Northumberland, initiated experiments towards the introduction of steam traction; and with him two men became prominently associated. One was William Hedley, the colliery viewer or manager, and the other was Timothy Hackworth, at that time the foreman blacksmith. An early outcome of their efforts was the so-called 'Grasshopper' type of locomotive, the first of which, completed in 1811, exemplified two features of great importance. Trevithick's Pen-y-Darran engine had only one cylinder, and a huge flywheel to carry the action over the dead centres at each end of the piston stroke. The Wylam 'Grasshopper' of 1811 had two cylinders, mounted vertically. They drove cranks at opposite ends of a horizontal shaft running parallel to, and between, the main axles of the locomotive. The arms of these cranks were set at right angles to each other, so that by this means the thrust from the two cylinders was continuous.

The method of transmitting the power from the cylinders to the cranks was weirdly primitive. The cylinders had a relatively long stroke and, to reduce this to what was needed to actuate the cranks, a huge scale-beam was used, pivoted on a triangular framework at the chimney end of the boiler. The boiler formed the centre piece of the whole affair, to which everything else was attached by bits and pieces of brackets and such like. Two hefty baulks of timber formed the cradle on which the boiler was carried, and the boiler itself had wooden cladding outside to minimise loss of heat by radiation. The crankshaft transmitted the drive to the two main axles through spur gearing.

The internals of the boiler were due to Hackworth, and involved his return flue system of heating. The firehole door was at the chimney end. This, and the chimney itself were placed side by side, and the flue ran the length of the boiler, made a U-turn, and came back to the chimney. The fireman, beside the chimney, rode on the coal and water tender. The driver was at the opposite end of the boiler. The water tank was of iron construction, and this seems to have

One of William Hedley's 'Grasshopper' locomotives (Crown Copyright).

been used on most of the locomotives on the colliery lines in Northumberland in very early days; though at the time of the Rainhill trials, in 1829, the water supply was carried in large barrels. This very historic locomotive is now on display at the Science Museum, South Kensington.

While the Wylam trio, Christopher Blackett, William Hedley and Timothy Hackworth were developing the 'Grasshopper' type, building later examples on eight instead of four wheels, to distribute the weight more evenly on the rough and indifferent track at the colliery, the men at Killingworth Colliery, a little to the north-east, were showing an increasing interest in what was going on. There, Nicholas Wood, the distinguished mining engineer, was viewer, and George Stephenson was enginewright. They both felt that there was every advantage to be gained from locomotive haulage, and were sure that they could do equally well anything that was then being done at Wylam. George Stephenson made a friend of Jonathan Foster, the enginewright at Wylam, and in his spare time was frequently there watching operations—to the great annoyance of Blackett and Hedley.

In the first Killingworth locomotive, completed in 1814, the cylinders having a stroke of two feet were on the vertical centre line of the boiler, and sunk half-way into it. The 'Grasshopper' gear was athwartships, instead of longitudinally as on the Wylam engines, and each cylinder drove on to a separate axle, again through spur gearing underneath the locomotive frame. But it was, of course, necessary to keep the strokes of the two cylinders properly in phase, and this was accomplished by linking the two driving gear wheels by a central pinion. It was an ingenious though intricate piece of machinery, requiring rather more precision in manufacture and assembly than the facilities of the Killingworth workshops could then manage, and one is not surprised that in his second locomotive, built in 1815, Stephenson abandoned the geared drive. Instead he fitted a crank pin to one of the spokes of the main driving wheel, and the lower end of the connecting rod was attached to this pin by a ball and socket joint. The cylinders, still half sunk into the boiler, were mounted immediately above each driving axle. In the centre of each axle was a toothed wheel, and over this

Stephenson & Losh's patent locomotive, 1816 (Timothy Hackworth and the locomotive).

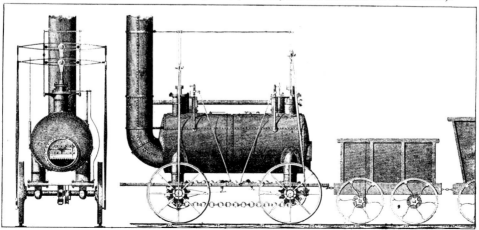

Stockton & Darlington Railway, Stephenson's Locomotion No 1 *of 1825, fitted with Hackworth's plug type wheels.*

passed a sprocket-chain, to maintain the correct phase relationship between the crank pins on the front and rear axles.

A very fine example of a Killingworth locomotive, for many years standing on a pedestal in Newcastle Central station, and now in the City Museum, Newcastle, shows very clearly the arrangement of the scale beam by which the piston rods were linked to the connecting rods. The locomotive, now preserved, is not quite in its original form in one respect to be mentioned later. But reverting to the gear on the top of the boiler it must be explained that the scale beams did not oscillate as on the Wylam 'Grasshoppers', but remained horizontal as they moved up and down in the pairs of vertical guides. They had crank pins on the wheels, as in Stephenson's first locomotive of 1814, but originally had chain and sprocket gears. The coupling rod between the two crank pins was a later addition. This latter was such a simple alternative to the chain arrangement for keeping the movements of the two cylinders and their gear in synchronisation that it is a little surprising that it was not adopted earlier. There is some controversy as to who introduced it.

In Warren's book, *A Century of Locomotive Building*, it is stated that the change was made 'after 1825', with the suggestion that it may have been due to Nicholas Wood; whereas in Robert Young's book, *Timothy Hackworth and the Locomotive*, the change is claimed for him. I think this is the more likely, because at the time of the opening of the Stockton and Darlington Railway, and début of the famous *Locomotion No. 1*, Hackworth had left Wylam Colliery and become locomotive superintendent of the S & D at Shildon. It was he also, as related in Chapter 13, who introduced the cast iron 'plug' type of wheel, which is incorporated in the working replica of *Locomotion*. It seems likely, therefore, that this pioneer locomotive had the sprocket gears and chain when she ran on the opening day of the Stockton and Darlington Railway in September 1825. She certainly had spoked wheels, and not the cast plug type, on that memorable occasion.

Chapter 3

The railway network of Great Britain— its growth, to zenith

The British railway system which grew, in a matter of 75 years, from the little Stockton and Darlington to a network that, in a density appropriate to population and industry, came to cover the entire country, was an organism that resulted wholly from individual, local and private enterprise. There was no master plan evolved by the central Government, no strategic considerations, no sociological grounds for overall planning. Unlike France, for example, where the whole country was neatly parcelled out between a few major companies, or North America where the Governments made free grants of land to encourage the building of railways to open up virgin territory, the British entrepreneurs had to go it alone—not that they would have wished it otherwise, because for most projects there was plenty of money available. Parliament certainly exercised a fairly stringent watching brief, though most of the opposition in the early days came from vested interests which saw no reason for any changes in the status quo, and resisted the intrusion of railways.

Much of the original growth was remarkably haphazard from an overall national viewpoint. Local interests promoted railways to serve their own business and social requirements. Rival interests put up schemes in opposition and, provided that the finance was sound, Parliament offered no objection. The principle of free enterprise was jealously guarded, and it was only if one company sought, by the absorption of lesser ones, to establish a monopoly in its own area that Parliament stepped in with a veto. As the network spread the prospect of great trunk lines gradually evolved. No objection was raised to lengthwise amalgamations, because these did not infringe upon the anti-monopoly principle; but, as in every other form of business enterprise, loopholes were found, and the resulting network which, by the year 1900, extended to no less than 20,000 miles of route, came to include many sections built in the white heat of 19th century competition that were really redundant. It is in tracing these lines and recalling their origin that much interest in an archaeological vein can be aroused. The track of a disused railway is not easy to obliterate. The research could take two forms: firstly, that of tracing the routes themselves with the guidance of a large-scale period Ordnance Survey map and secondly, endeavouring to establish the original ownership.

Before going into such detail, however, it is important to obtain a broad picture of how the railway network was built up. The year 1835 saw a great amount of planning and projecting of railways in the north-east. Further south three great trunk lines had been projected which, if authorised and eventually completed, would provide a continuous line of railway from London to Leeds. These were the London and Birmingham, which had already secured its Act of Incorporation; the Midland Counties, which began from a junction with Birmingham line at Rugby, and continued through Leicester to Derby, and then there was the North Midland, carrying the line northward to Leeds. Both these latter companies were incorporated in 1836 and the complete chain was opened to traffic by 1840. The planning in the north-east, however, began in Darlington from local men who felt that the interests of any major north to south line, connecting up with the projected railways south of Leeds, would be better served by indigenous investment rather than that of remote, albeit wealthy, projectors from the south. So emanated, in 1835, the conception of a Great North of England Railway, with Darlington as its focal point and running south to York and northwards to Newcastle. Joseph Pease of the great Quaker family, son of Edward—greatest of the 'founding fathers' of the Stockton & Darlington Railway—was the mainspring of this enterprise; but at the same time a formidable rival was in the ascendant at York.

George Hudson, then no more than a linen draper, but a forceful and far-seeing character, saw the possibility of furthering the trade of the city by establishing a railway connection with the south. So the York and North Midland Railway was promoted, to join up with the North Midland itself near Normanton. Success bred success and with amalgamations, promotions and take-overs, Hudson was eventually in control of a railway 'empire' that extended from Rugby and Bristol in the south to Berwick-on-Tweed—not that the territories were exclusive to his companies. There were rivals in several key areas that he sought to smother with additional lines of his own. He fought tooth and nail to block the projection of a direct line from London to York, which would take traffic from his line from Rugby via Leicester, Derby and Chesterfield. It was the initial success of his numerous schemes that was one of the major factors in sparking off the railway mania of the later 1840s, in which the investing public went railway mad. Here, however, I am not so much concerned with the inevitable crash, and of his own disgrace and disappearance following the revelation of certain fraudulent practices, as of the physical assets that resulted. And they were immense.

In 1850, the year after the fall of Hudson, the main line was completed through from York to Berwick, there connecting with the North British Railway, to Edinburgh, while his York and North Midland had extended to Scarborough and taken leases of the Leeds and Selby, and of the Selby and Hull. Meanwhile the Leeds Northern, promoted originally as the Leeds and Thirsk, and a rival to the Great North of England, had remained a thorn in his side, while the Stockton and Darlington had remained resolutely independent. This latter secured, moreover, control of an important east to west line across the Pennines, known as the South Durham and Lancashire Union and running from Barnard Castle via Kirkby Stephen to a junction with the Lancaster and Carlisle Railway at Tebay, in Westmorland. This line was, however, a mere infant company compared to the pioneer east to west railway of the whole country—the Newcastle and Carlisle—the Act of Incorporation of which was passed by Parliament as long previously as 1829.

In the year 1850 the railway situation in the north-east can be appreciated from the accompanying map, which shows the main lines and more important branches of the five railways in the area: *a*) York, Newcastle and Berwick, *b*)

York and North Midland, *c*) Leeds Northern, *d*) Stockton and Darlington and *e*) Newcastle and Carlisle. The first three amalgamated to form the North Eastern Railway in 1854, and this large combine absorbed the Newcastle and Carlisle in 1862 and the Stockton and Darlington in 1863. The latter company had absorbed the South Durham and Lancashire Union in 1862.

Tracing now Hudson's one-time empire south of Leeds, the North Midland, engineered by George Stephenson, was a magnificent through route to the south and one can well imagine with what envious eyes Hudson looked upon it, until he secured control. It was curious, however, that in planning a splendid direct line it by-passed two of the largest centres of population, Wakefield and Sheffield. Stephenson was clearly following his basic principles of securing easy gradients and, to avoid the very hilly country to the south of Sheffield, he eschewed the place altogether and kept at river level along the Rother valley to Chesterfield thence, after the long Clay Cross tunnel, passing through beautiful country to reach Derby. The southward continuation, to join the London and Birmingham at Rugby, was engineered by that stormy petrel among British railway pioneers, C.B. Vignoles. The third constituent of the great amalgamation of 1844 that formed the Midland Railway was the Birmingham and Derby Junction, and the Birmingham and Gloucester, and the Bristol and Gloucester were absorbed soon afterwards.

The build-up of the West Coast main line embracing the various companies eventually embodied in the London and North Western Railway, had begun much earlier, and can be traced back to the outstanding success of the first-ever Inter-City railway, the Liverpool and Manchester. Though no more than a relatively short run of 31 miles, its character stemmed from the 'mixed' nature of its traffic—passengers in their thousands, as well as freight of every kind. No more than three years after the Liverpool and Manchester had opened for business, two new companies were incorporated to construct between them nearly 190 miles of railway, to link London with the mid-point of the L & M, at Newton Junction. These two companies were the London and Birmingham, and the Grand Junction. Both opened for business in 1837 and it then became possible to travel by train all the way from London to Liverpool and Manchester. The City of Birmingham is a geographical curiosity in that it is built on no navigable river, nor in a valley, but on the crest of a hill, and its first passenger station, Curzon Street, was built at the foot of the hill. It was a terminus for both London and Birmingham and for Grand Junction trains.

A rival to the Grand Junction for northbound traffic from Birmingham was incorporated in 1837 in the shape of the Manchester and Birmingham Railway; but it was built no further south than Crewe, where its traffic fed into the Grand Junction. Before the major amalgamation of 1846, by which the London and North Western Railway was formed, the Grand Junction had absorbed the Liverpool and Manchester, the Chester and Crewe, and a most important link, not yet completed, the Trent Valley Railway. Unlike the Hudson philosophy, which considered that as long as there was any line of rails that was all the communication that was needed, the men of the Grand Junction saw, at an

Maps on following pages
Page 32 *Railways in North Eastern England, 1850.* **Page 33** *The main network of the Midland Railway at the fall of George Hudson.* **Page 34** *The London & North Western, as formed by amalgamation, in 1846.*

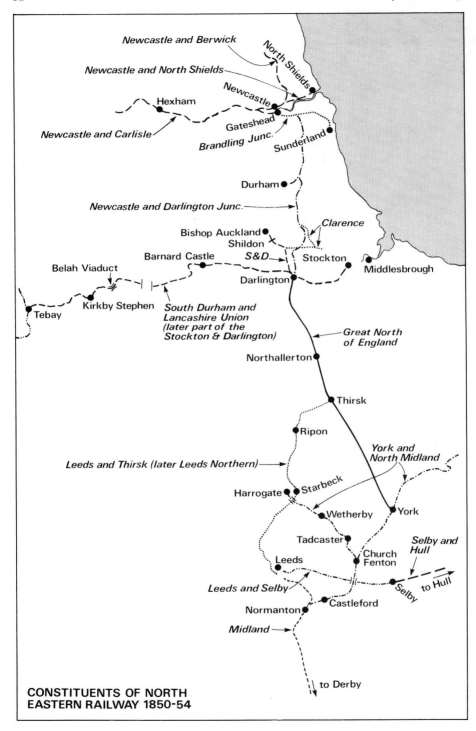

Newcastle and Berwick

Newcastle and North Shields

North Shields

Newcastle and North Shields

Newcastle

Hexham

Gateshead

Newcastle and Carlisle

Brandling Junc.

Sunderland

Durham

Newcastle and Darlington Junc.

Clarence

Bishop Auckland
Shildon

Barnard Castle

S&D

Stockton

Belah Viaduct

Darlington

Middlesbrough

Tebay

Kirkby Stephen

*South Durham and
Lancashire Union
(later part of the
Stockton & Darlington)*

*Great North
of England*

Northallerton

Thirsk

Ripon

Leeds and Thirsk (later Leeds Northern)

*York and
North Midland*

Harrogate

Starbeck

Wetherby

York

Tadcaster

*Selby and
Hull*

Leeds

Church
Fenton

Leeds and Selby

Selby

to Hull

Normanton

Castleford

Midland

to Derby

**CONSTITUENTS OF NORTH
EASTERN RAILWAY 1850-54**

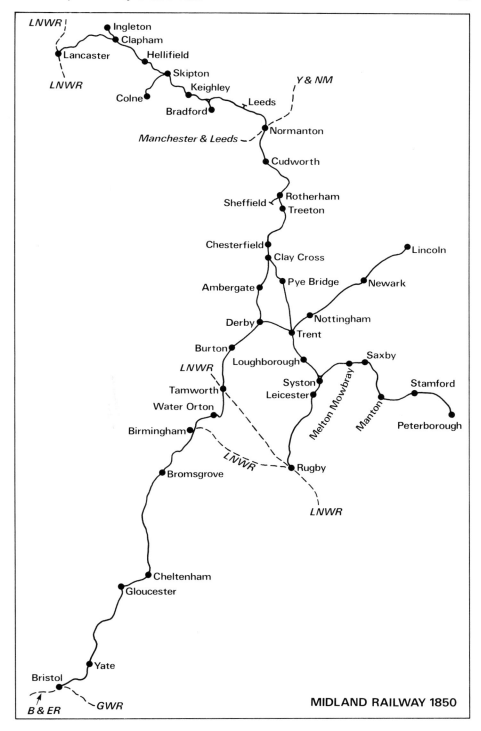

LNWR

Ingleton
Clapham
Hellifield
Lancaster
Skipton
LNWR
Keighley
Colne
Bradford
Leeds
Y & NM
Manchester & Leeds
Normanton
Cudworth
Rotherham
Sheffield
Treeton
Chesterfield
Lincoln
Clay Cross
Pye Bridge
Ambergate
Newark
Derby
Nottingham
Trent
Burton
Saxby
Loughborough
LNWR
Syston
Stamford
Tamworth
Leicester
Water Orton
Melton Mowbray
Manton
Birmingham
Peterborough
LNWR
Bromsgrove
Rugby

LNWR

Cheltenham
Gloucester

Yate
Bristol
B & ER — *GWR*

MIDLAND RAILWAY 1850

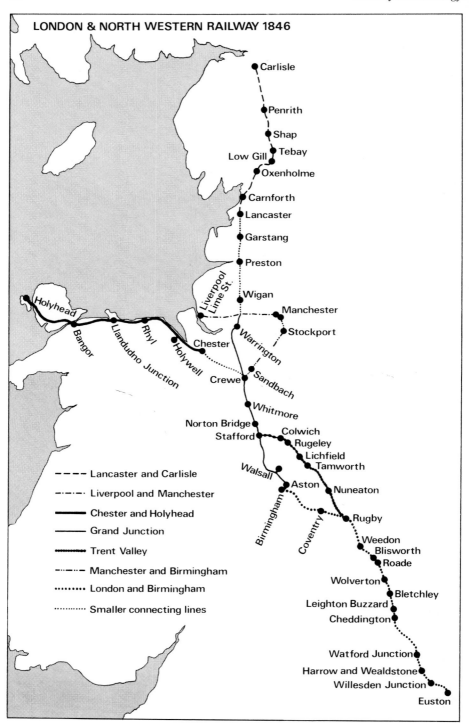

LONDON & NORTH WESTERN RAILWAY 1846

Carlisle

Penrith

Shap

Tebay

Low Gill

Oxenholme

Carnforth

Lancaster

Garstang

Preston

Liverpool Lime St.

Wigan

Manchester

Stockport

Holyhead

Bangor

Llandudno Junction

Rhyl

Holywell

Chester

Warrington

Crewe

Sandbach

Whitmore

Norton Bridge

Stafford

Colwich

Rugeley

Lichfield

Tamworth

Walsall

Aston

Nuneaton

Birmingham

Coventry

Rugby

Weedon

Blisworth

Roade

Wolverton

Bletchley

Leighton Buzzard

Cheddington

Watford Junction

Harrow and Wealdstone

Willesden Junction

Euston

– – – Lancaster and Carlisle

–·–·– Liverpool and Manchester

━━━ Chester and Holyhead

─── Grand Junction

▪▪▪▪▪ Trent Valley

–··–·· Manchester and Birmingham

········· London and Birmingham

·········· Smaller connecting lines

early date, that for the through north-south connection, that link up at Curzon Street in Birmingham with its reversal of direction, was going to be a crippling handicap. Instead they sponsored a direct line southwards from Stafford to Rugby, which tapped the important towns of Lichfield, Tamworth and Nuneaton en route.

So, when the London and Birmingham, the Grand Junction, and the Manchester and Birmingham Railways joined forces in 1846 they had, with their associated and ultimately absorbed lines to the north and west, an extensive system. The northern connections included two very famous railways—the Chester and Holyhead, with its magnificently historic tubular bridges, and the great harbour works at Holyhead itself, and the ever fascinating Lancaster and Carlisle, with its mountain climbing amid the wild country of the Westmorland fells. Another useful constituent of the L & NWR was the Leeds, Dewsbury and Manchester, putting the important town of Huddersfield on to the railway map.

Among the great men of railway pioneering days the name of Brunel stands apart from all others—not above, or below, yet utterly different. In the north-east Hudson is remembered kindly for his greater, rather than his less-reputable, achievements. Robert Stephenson and Joseph Locke are giants of international fame; but Brunel has a very special niche in the west country, where every achievement of his is revered. Having persuaded the original board of the Great Western Railway to adopt the broad gauge, 7 foot $\frac{1}{4}$ inch, he set out by super-lative engineering to build a road that once seen would convince all others that they must do the same. Only his estimates of human nature were wrong. The Stephensons, Locke, Hudson and all the others just dug in, adamant in their opposition; but even before the major confrontation of the Gauge War was over, and the lengthy sittings of the Royal Commission set up to try and resolve the gathering *impasse*, Brunel had carried the broad gauge to Bristol by 1840, on to Exeter by 1844, to Plymouth by 1848, and right through South Wales to Swansea by 1850. At its maximum extent it had reached Penzance, Weymouth, Milford Haven and Wolverhampton.

It was a magnificent conception, magnificently executed; but it was fore-doomed to extinction. The Great Western Railway could not exist as a tight little entity on its own. It absorbed narrow-gauge lines of its own like the Oxford, Worcester and Wolverhampton. There had to be interchange with the narrow gauge at stations like Basingstoke, Gloucester and Hereford, not to mention the most northerly point of all, Wolverhampton. Nevertheless, in building his broad gauge system, in its track, locomotives, signalling and, above all, in his majestic major works of civil engineering, Brunel bequeathed upon posterity, and especially on students of railway history and archaeology, a richer store of memories and priceless documentation perhaps than any other one man in the whole saga of railways.

Had the proprietors of the Bristol and Exeter Railway been more discerning the whole of the west of England, beyond a diagonal line running from Basingstoke to Dorchester, could have been sealed off against any advances of narrow gauge lines. Having projected a two-pronged drive from Reading to the south and west—the 'Berks and Hants'—to Newbury in the first county and Basingstoke in the second, Brunel developed the idea of an Exeter Great Western Railway: a direct line to the west avoiding the long perambulation via Swindon, Bath and Bristol. It was conceived in the same way as the men of the Grand Junction had sponsored the Trent Valley line, to avoid the detour and

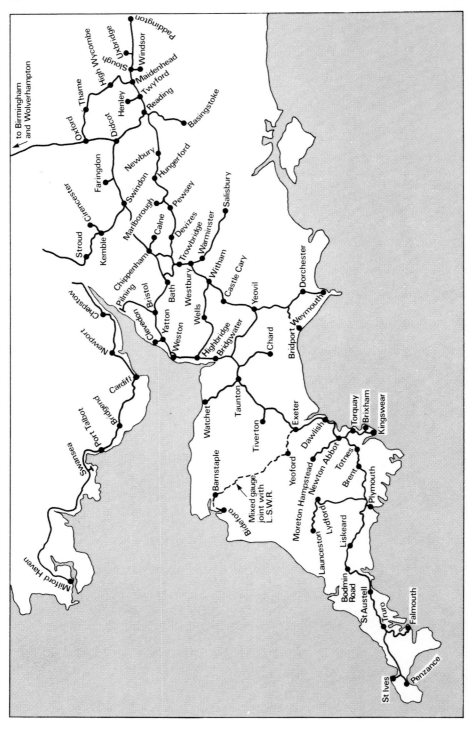

Opposite *The maximum extent of the broad gauge on the Great Western.* **Above** *Broad gauge in South Wales: Brunel's station at Bridgend.*

traffic complications of Birmingham and the Black Country. The Exeter Great Western would have passed through Hungerford, Frome, Yeovil, Crewkerne and Honiton; but the Bristol and Exeter people feared that it would drain off some of their traffic, and they secured the rejection of the Bill when it was presented to Parliament. This left the way clear for the London and South Western.

This latter originated as a straightforward, finely engineered, direct line from London to Southampton, of which Joseph Locke was the principal architect. When, by the rejection of Brunel's 'Exeter Great Western' project, the country west of Basingstoke was left wide open, except for a rather half-hearted broad-gauge line known as the Wilts, Somerset and Weymouth, the South Western eventually built their own line from Basingstoke to Exeter. Unlike some of the railways in the Midlands and the north east, capital was not readily forthcoming and it was not until 1860 that Exeter was reached. Locke again was the engineer, and the 88 miles between Salisbury and Exeter in its superb alignment of sharply undulating gradients, was typical of his constructional philosophy of avoiding tunnels wherever possible. Locke had more than a purely professional interest in this line because he was MP for Honiton. It became one of the most exciting lines in the country for high speed travel when it was necessary to go hard down hill in order to gain impetus for climbing the next steep ascent.

Locke's abhorrence of tunnels no doubt came from the grisly task he had to take over on the half finished line between Manchester and Sheffield. The first proposals for a railway between these two towns was made as early as 1830, but the Act of Incorporation for what was at first known as the Sheffield, Ashton-under-Lyne, and Manchester Railway was not secured until May 1837. Vignoles

A typical Brunellian wayside station at Pangbourne. Strange to see a wagon on the up line, standing nonchalantly, without any immediate junction.

was the first engineer and he essayed the tremendous task of boring the great tunnel under the crest of the Pennine Range 3 miles and 22 yards long beneath Woodhead Moor. Largely through his own exuberance and his somewhat volatile nature, he was soon in difficulties and, in December 1839, he resigned and was replaced by Locke. To save expense the original tunnel was made single-tracked, and such were the difficulties in construction that it was not until December 1845 that the line was opened for traffic. That single line bore soon proved to be a case of false economy. It quickly proved an acute bottleneck and, as early as 1847, work was commenced on a second bore alongside. Although on its completion the *Sheffield Iris* newspaper hailed it as '. . . a wondrous triumph of art over nature', the drivers and firemen who had to work through soon began to have other ideas!

One cannot take the gradual build-up of the British railway network in strict chronological order, and actually there were two other early lines crossing from Lancashire into Yorkshire, one of which preceded the Woodhead route by several years. The Leeds, Dewsbury and Manchester has already been mentioned in the build up of the London and North Western Railway. This was opened for traffic in 1849 and included a tunnel at its summit, Standedge, that was of exactly the same length at Woodhead, but which was wisely made for a double track at the outset. At the summit of the steep ascent from the Manchester side the track is level, and in later steam days advantage was taken of this to install water troughs—the only ones *inside a tunnel* to be found anywhere in the world. The first Trans-Pennine route, however, was the Manchester and Leeds, authorised in 1836 and opened throughout in 1841, and later forming the west-east backbone of the Lancashire and Yorkshire Railway. Although it included, almost inevitably, a long tunnel under the great dividing mountain chain the gradients were much easier than on either of the rival

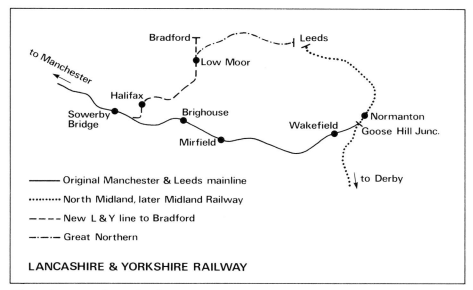

The early approaches to Leeds.

routes. After going almost due north from Manchester to pass through Rochdale the line emerged from the summit tunnel to run at river level grades down the picturesque Vale of Todmorden. At its eastern end the line went into Leeds by the backway, as it were, continuing down the Calder Valley, through Wakefield to join the North Midland Railway at a place about half a mile south of Normanton called Goose Hill Junction.

The men of the London and North Western at one time hoped to keep Euston as the one departure point in London for the Midlands, the north-east and Scotland, as well as for their own territories; but there was a need for a fast direct route from London to York, and this was in part fulfilled in 1850 by the opening of the Great Northern Railway between Doncaster and the spectacular new terminus at Kings Cross, completed two years after the trains had started to run. North of Peterborough there were to be two alternative routes, and it was the Lincolnshire loop via Spalding, Boston and Lincoln itself that was ready first, and for two years provided the new trunk route to the north. The direct line via Grantham and Newark, which came to be one of the fastest lines in the world, was completed two years later. North of Doncaster the Great Northern trains proceeded very much 'by your leave', by running powers over the Lancashire and Yorkshire to Knottingly, and then from Ferrybridge on to the York and North Midland line. The direct North Eastern line southwards through Selby, was not constructed until 1871.

Although the opening of the Great Northern Railway introduced a serious rival to Euston interests, so far as Anglo-Scottish traffic was concerned, it was an even greater embarrassment to the Midland. Hudson's second 'empire', so true to its name, now found itself hemmed in on both sides, with the Great Northern tapping a good deal of its former traffic. Cross-country lines originally thrown out to intersect and impede the new route were tending to act as feeders to it, and the need was felt for a second outlet to the south, other than over the heavily congested London and North Western, from Rugby. The first step to overcome this situation was to build a line southwards from Leicester through Market Harborough and Kettering to Bedford, and to continue south-eastwards to a trailing junction with the Great Northern at Hitchin. The latter company was ready enough to grant running powers to the Midland, as the tolls for a heavy traffic were likely to bring in a substantial revenue. But the result was serious congestion on the line between Hitchin and Kings Cross, with the Midland naturally coming off second best, and paying through the nose for it! The answer was the building of an independent line from Bedford to London, completed in 1868.

Meanwhile, as a result of amalgamations of various one-time independent companies, the railway map of East Anglia showed the Great Eastern in very nearly undisputed possession. Partly because most of the traffic was agricultural and partly because capital was not so readily available, nothing in the way of competitive lines were built, and the amalgamation of 1862 which brought the four principal lines in the area together, taking the name Great Eastern, produced a neatly integrated main line network with little or nothing in the way of potentially redundant lines. Across the northern part of Norfolk there ran the picturesque Midland and Great Northern Joint Railway. One of the most important sources of traffic was the Great Eastern and Great Northern Joint Line northward from March over which a great volume of coal traffic flowed from the Yorkshire pits into East Anglia and East London.

The Great Eastern had a very important connection from Bishopsgate, via the Thames Tunnel to the southern lines at New Cross, with direct running junctions on to both the Brighton and the South Eastern lines. One would not imagine that the projecting of an apparently straightforward railway like that from London to Brighton would give rise to much controversy but, believe it or not, there were at one time no fewer than six different routes proposed. There were complications also at the London end because it was expedient to use the tracks of the Greenwich Railway—the first ever to be built in London—for the first mile out of London Bridge, and next there was the Croydon Railway, already under construction. The Brighton line came to excel in picturesque names for its stations and signal boxes and, when the main line was finalised, the southern end of the Croydon Railway was at 'Jolly Sailor'! Next, the South Eastern Railway had been authorised to build its main line from Redhill eastwards to Folkestone and Dover, and, from Stoats Nest—another lovely name!—southwards to Redhill, the line to Brighton would be owned by the South Eastern. The remarkable jumble of ownerships of track included in the $50\frac{3}{4}$-mile run from London to Brighton, where there was a signal box named Lovers Walk, was thus:

Section	Distance Miles	Ownership
London Bridge-Corbett's Lane	$1\frac{1}{2}$	Greenwich
Corbett's Lane-Jolly Sailor	$6\frac{3}{4}$	Croydon
Jolly Sailor-Stoats Nest	$6\frac{1}{4}$	London-Brighton
Stoats Nest-Redhill	$6\frac{1}{4}$	South Eastern
Redhill-Brighton	30	London-Brighton

Opposite *The Great Eastern at its maximum extent.*

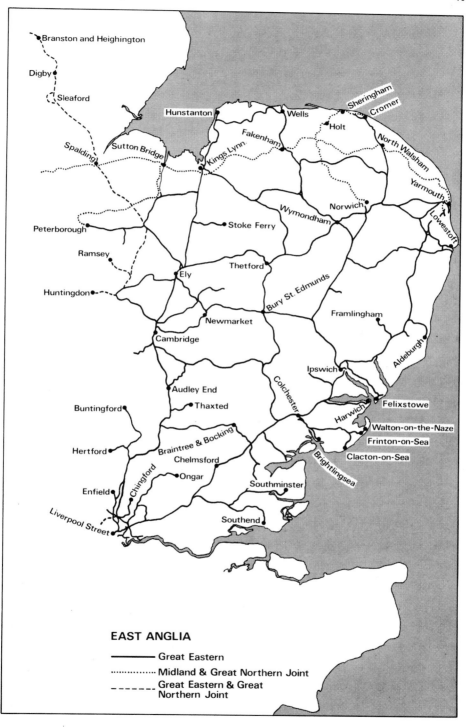

EAST ANGLIA

————— Great Eastern

············· Midland & Great Northern Joint

— — — — Great Eastern & Great
Northern Joint

The line was opened throughout in 1841. East of that ultimately very direct line from London to Brighton, railway construction developed into one of the most astonishing 'free for all' contests ever witnessed in Great Britain. When the South Eastern Railway built its remarkable straight main line from Redhill to Dover, through the very heart of Kent, and began throwing off useful branches to Maidstone, Hastings and Canterbury, it would have seemed that they were well on the way to a very snug monopoly, especially as by an extension of the Greenwich line they tapped the Thames-side area through Gravesend and, by purchase of what had been a canal tunnel, got through to Strood and the Medway towns. The access to certain places was, however, distinctly round about, of which Deal, from Dover, was one classic example and the need to reverse direction in Ramsgate to get to Margate, another. One way or another the County of Kent was reasonably well covered by the year 1850. It was, however, the desire of people in the Medway towns to have a direct line to Faversham, Canterbury and Dover that formed the starting point of the financially unstable venture, which before long rocked the South Eastern to its foundations. Here I am not concerned with the chaotic business affairs of the London, Chatham and Dover Railway, but only of the lines that were built to antagonise and embarrass the South Eastern at every end and turn. But the surprising thing is that, when the most bellicose of their respective leaders had gone and the two companies agreed to work together under a single managing committee, very little adjustment and connectional lines were necessary to provide the County of Kent with a finely integrated railway system.

The Midland Railway, probing towards north-western and Scottish outlets, had reached Skipton by 1847 and Ingleton by 1849 and, from the moorland Clapham Junction in the north-west of Yorkshire, it had a line through to Lancaster by 1850. The beautifully situated dale town of Ingleton became a

The situation in Kent, 1852: the South Eastern in an apparent monopoly.

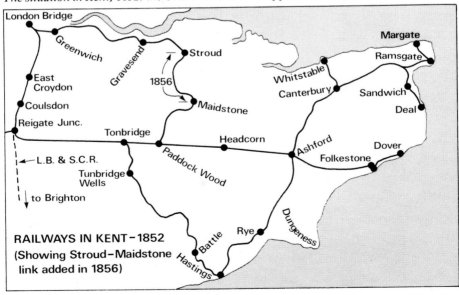

RAILWAYS IN KENT – 1852
(Showing Stroud–Maidstone link added in 1856)

storm centre of railway politics in mid-Victorian times. The line thence to Skipton was originally that of an independent company, the North Western, usually referred to as the 'Little' North Western, to distinguish from the L & NWR; and the Midland, seeing in it a convenient springboard for an advance towards Scotland, proposed an extension up the Lune valley to join the London and North Western at Low Gill. The latter company countered this by building a line of their own to a head-on confrontation at Ingleton. The game of railway politics was then played for all it was worth, making things as awkward as possible for the Midland; with the result that the latter company decided to build a completely independent line to Carlisle. This, one of the grandest express routes in England, the ever-famous Settle and Carlisle, was opened in 1876.

In bringing the Midland Railway to the Scottish Border I have drawn nearly a quarter century out of chronological order, because it was in the late 1840s that the enterprise of the Grand Junction Railway, following the successful projection of its protégé, the Lancaster and Carlisle, sent their great engineer, Joseph Locke, northward from Carlisle to find the most suitable route to both Glasgow and Edinburgh. English interests were prominently involved, not less in the prospect of having a powerful rival route to that of the East Coast companies from London to Edinburgh. The Grand Junction and their allies at Euston felt that they should secure the route to Glasgow entirely for themselves. There was much sparring for position. In Scotland itself the Glasgow, Paisley, Kilmarnock and Ayr Railway had been in operation for several years and Glasgow interests were adamant that the line to the south should be a continuation of their railway, by Mauchline and Cumnock into the valley of the Nith and Dumfries. But Locke recommended a line up Annandale rather than Nithsdale, because by then climbing over the watershed into Upper Clydesdale he would not only get a shorter route to Glasgow, but by forking at Carstairs he would get an equally good route to Edinburgh. The GPK & A people could not have cared less about Edinburgh, and were furious when the Annandale route was preferred and authorised, as the Caledonian Railway. But although their own line, through Dumfries and Annan, was authorised soon after, and completed to a junction with the Caledonian at Gretna in 1850, the two routes remained deadly rivals until both were merged into the London Midland and Scottish system in 1923.

The line to the north was continued, from junctions in the Motherwell and Coatbridge area, by a chain of independent companies, all of which were eventually absorbed into the Caledonian, and which took the line through Larbert, Stirling, Perth, Forfar and Stonehaven to Aberdeen. The 'Granite City' was reached in 1850, and the line throughout from Carlisle became owned by the Caledonian from 1866. Rivalry from the East Coast group of lines was at first inhibited by the need for crossing the estuaries of the Forth and Tay, and the first attempt to bridge the latter ended in a disaster of unparalleled magnitude in 1879. It was not until a new Tay Bridge had been built and the magnificent triple-cantilevered Forth Bridge was completed in 1891 that the East Coast route could run on anything like equality between London and Aberdeen.

In the mountain vastnesses, beyond the 'Highland Line'—a geographical rather than a railway line in this case—some of the most fascinating railways in the whole of the British Isles were enterprised, more for sociological reasons

Hebridean outpost of the Highland Railway: the station and pier at Kyle of Lochalsh, with the hills of Skye across the water.

than for any thoughts of immediate profits to the investors. It is indeed unlikely that those who built the chain of single line railways, extending from near Perth to Wick and Thurso, envisaged that there would be a time when the Highland Railway would prove a strategic lifeline of the utmost importance, not only to Great Britain, but to the Grand Alliance of 1914-8. One needs only to utter the words Scapa Flow! The long branch line to the Kyle of Lochalsh was another strategic route in those anxious years.

The Callander and Oban Railway came to be a much enjoyed tourist route, so much so that the Caledonian Railway had built a sumptuous Pullman observation car, from which the mountain panoramas could be enjoyed to the utmost; but the line that has always appealed perhaps more to the imagintion than any other is the West Highland, making a winding and mountainous way from Craigendoran, on the Firth of Clyde to Fort William. The continuation, over the Mallaig Extension, completed in 1901, goes through what was once described as 'an outstandingly harsh piece of country'. For those who love the wild, however, this line has a sublime quality not easily described, with some distant and appealing sights of the Hebridean islands towards its western end.

This is not much more than an outline sketch of the British railway network. There are some parts of it not yet mentioned that will come in for detailed study later, such as the valleys of South Wales, the Furness district of Cumbria and the tangled skeins of disused and near-forgotten routes where rationalisation of traffic flows, following nationalisation, has led to many closures. But the scene is now set for a first exploration.

Chapter 4

Tracing abandoned routes

The route mileage of the British railways reached its maximum around 1910, since when there have been substantial reductions. In entering upon the subject of abandoned routes it could be very easy to become involved in discussions about the ethics, or economics of this or that closure, or to voice one's astonishment that even south of the geographical Highland Line there are now some very large areas, including considerable centres of industry and population that are completely bereft of railways. That, however, would be to become diverted from the purpose of this book, which is to seek out what remains, and then try to build up a picture of what has gone before. With the national route mileage reduced by some 40 per cent of its former maximum it would obviously be impossible to refer to every abandoned line; so I have taken a few, of which I have personal knowledge of past days, to discuss what can be seen now and deduced from it.

A great deal of preliminary work can be done from a study of maps. Unlike the subjects of much archaeological research the routes of railways were well documented, while the current editions of the one-inch Ordnance Survey maps usually mark the track of abandoned lines. But the original *raison d'être* of many of these is not readily apparent from a careful study of the track itself, or of any surviving structure, and the purely physical study needs to be supplemented and enriched by investigations into usage and ownership. To this end another series of maps can be invaluable. Before the nationalisation of the railways in 1948, the dividing and adjusting of traffic receipts as between the companies involved for a 'two-company', 'three-company'— or more—route was done by the Railway Clearing House. For this it was essential to have precise details of the mileages involved and the exact junction points. These were provided in a most comprehensive series of junction diagrams, covering every junction in the British Isles where more than one company was involved. The massive volumes containing upwards of 150 sheets are fascinating and invaluable aids to a study of the railway system of the past. Although they were never available to the public they can now be seen in major reference libraries, and in the Records Office at Kew.

Some of these maps are extraordinarily interesting in showing how, in days long past, the major railways had wholly owned depots and short lengths of track far from any part of the parent systems. Who would imagine nowadays that the Midland Railway had a coal depot beside Kensington High Street station, on the Inner Circle, and another at Lillie Bridge, in West Kensington?

One wonders how loaded coal wagons from the Midland main line were worked round to these relatively inaccessible depots. The traffic would be welcome enough once it got there. I myself have a vague, though unconfirmed recollection of having seen Midland 0-6-0 tank engines in the coal yard at Kensington High Street. It needs no fewer than three RCH maps to trace the route. Proceeding south over the Midland's own line from Cricklewood to Acton Wells a load of coal would then continue over the North & South Western Junction line (jointly owned by the L & NW, Midland and North London Railways) to South Acton, and there, passing on to the London & South Western, making a wide sweep to the east, to proceed over tracks now familiar as London Transport (but then owned by the L & SWR) to Studland Road Junction just east of Ravenscourt Park, where it passed on to the District Line, and so on to our present map. In so doing there would be tolls to be paid to the London and North Western, the London and South Western, the North London and to the Metropolitan District! Because of the intense occupation of the line between Turnham Green and Earls Court by District trains, even in steam days, the Midland coal trains would have to work their way round from Cricklewood in the night, with their engines more or less impounded in Kensington till the next night.

Another interesting case of an isolated goods depot on the eastern boundary

Midland Railway: depots in South and West Kensington (1899), and the access lines.

of the City of London was the quarter mile of London and North Western property leading from the Great Eastern, near Fenchurch Street, to Haydon Square. Before coming to recall how freight traffic from the North Western managed to make its way to Haydon Square I must tell also over what very historic ground the modern electric trains of Eastern Region bustle in and out of Fenchurch Street. The line was originally that of the London and Blackwall, no more than three miles long, and worked by *cable*; but when it was opened in 1840 the gauge was 5 feet $\frac{1}{2}$ inch. Cable operation did not prove very reliable, and when the time came for this quite strategic piece of railway to be linked up with the growing network in East London, and a branch was projected from Stepney to Bow, the gauge was changed to the standard 4 feet $8\frac{1}{2}$ inches, and locomotive haulage introduced. The change was made in 1849 in time to link up, at Bow, with the elaborately styled East and West India Docks and Birmingham Junction Railway. This latter was from the outset associated with the London and North Western, and Robert Stephenson was the engineer. It soon became much better known under the name it assumed in 1853, the North London.

From this the line of connection to Haydon Square becomes clear. The North London secured running powers for freight over the Blackwall line, from Bow, and the L & NWR built the short connecting line, just short of the terminus at Fenchurch Street into the wholly owned goods depot. There is an amusing story of early days at Haydon Square. Traffic was booming and more space was needed. On one side of the property there were then some very fine old trees. Word got round among the local residents that these were to be felled to make more track space, and a strong conservation movement started. Many signatures to a petition were obtained, and a deputation waited upon Charles Edward Stewart, Secretary of the L & NWR, at Euston and an ultimatum delivered: if he would not spare the trees a petition would be presented to Parliament. Stewart listened politely to their argument, but would give no promise; so off they went to Westminster. Just as promptly Stewart set off for Haydon Square, with an axe, and long before the deputation had made their submission the trees were down!

From goods depots tucked away at unexpected places in London there is an interesting field of exploration in the Isle of Thanet where the one time rivalry of the South Eastern Railway with the London Chatham and Dover left some very awkward track layouts, in Margate and Ramsgate. These remained unchanged for many years after the setting up of the Managing Committee for co-ordinating the affairs of the two companies in 1898. The South Eastern was first into the area, and the branch line from Ashford reached a terminus in Ramsgate in 1846. Very little thought seems to have been given to expeditious train working, because instead of taking the obvious course and continuing the line round to the north and making the terminus at Margate, a branch line was built from Ramsgate which trailed in, so that if one wanted to travel, say from Ashford to Margate, the train took one into Ramsgate first, then reversed direction, and proceeded sedately down the remaining $3\frac{1}{2}$ miles to the aptly named Margate Sands station, also a terminus. As a boy of about six years old I have vivid recollections of the tedium of a journey from Reading to and from Margate, and of the porters at Minster shouting 'over the bridge for Sandwich and Deal'.

The *Chatham* came into Thanet along the North Kent coast, along the line now electrified; but, having passed through Broadstairs, the environment of the

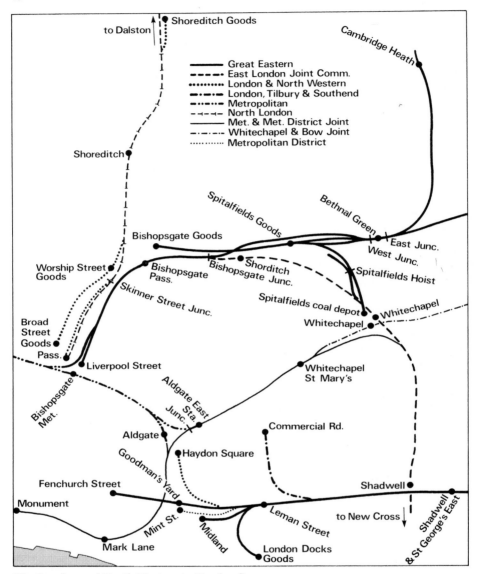

The London and North Western in Haydon Square.

South Eastern in Ramsgate was studiously avoided and the line tunnelled down almost to sea level to a terminus literally on the beach adjacent to Ramsgate Harbour. It was a prestigious affair, with an all-over roof, which blended in reasonably well with the usual aspect of a popular pleasure beach in Victorian times. It remained in service until 1926, when the Southern Railway completely remodelled the lines in the Thanet area. The site of Ramsgate Harbour station became an amusement park, but the tunnel leading up to the higher ground had an unexpected turn of usefulness during the Second World War, when it became a much appreciated municipal air raid shelter. Apart from the tunnel the tracks of the abandoned lines in Thanet can be clearly traced out on a one inch Ordnance Survey map. In later steam days Ramsgate became a major motive power depot for working trains to London via both the former Chatham and South Eastern routes.

In Thanet the lines that have been abandoned, though significant from the operating point, involve very little mileage. It is otherwise in the city near which I have been living now for more than 30 years—Bath. The Somerset and Dorset Joint was in itself a remarkable railway, but its connection with the Midland at Bath, and that company's connections with other lines farther north, made it an artery of much importance for through traffic from the north into so popular a holiday resort as Bournemouth. Unfortunately the very characteristics that made the Somerset and Dorset such an attractive line from the viewpoint of railway enthusiasts imposed a virtual stranglehold upon any chances of making it into an effective unit of modern transportation. Its freight business was not heavy and passenger traffic could rise to embarrassing heights in the peak of the summer season. At other times it was light; and, with the great increase in private family motoring in the 1950s, even the peak traffic dwindled sadly.

The Chatham and the South Eastern in Thanet.

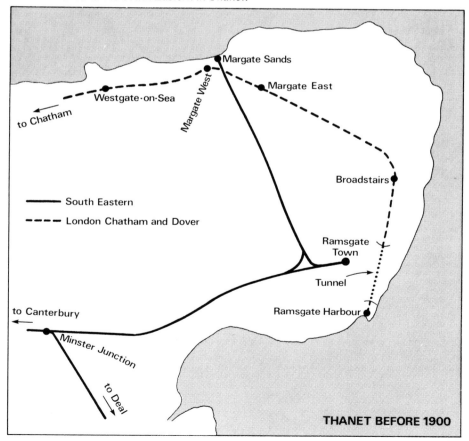

Ramsgate Harbour (David & Charles Ltd).

The crux of the matter was that by no means could the passenger service be brought up to acceptable modern standards of speed. But putting economics and the inevitability of closure on one side, what remains? There are many locations where railways were built on roundabout courses to avoid steep gradients, but leaving Bath by the Somerset and Dorset was like going up the side of a house! Looking at the track of that extraordinary line in a modern context one wonders if consideration was ever given to continuing north-east from Midford and trailing into the Trowbridge line of the Great Western, near Limpley Stoke. In 1874, when the extension line from the south was constructed, the Great Western branch down the valley of the Midford Brook had not been thought of and the Somerset and Dorset would have had the field to themselves. But there was another factor that undoubtedly influenced the Somerset and Dorset towards making a line into Bath that was independent of the Great Western, and that was they had eyes upon a connection with the Midland, in Bath, and the development of traffic from the north over their line to Bournemouth. So they went it alone.

The result was a four-mile stretch of railway that could well be described as the most difficult to operate on any main line in the British Isles. Money was short; various financial 'fiddles' were adopted in order to pay the contractors, and the line through a very hilly piece of country was not only built on no more than a single track, but the tunnels were made to the narrowest cross section that was possible. Although it is now some years since the line was closed to traffic and the track lifted, the Devonshire and Combe Down tunnels remain today as mute and poignant witnesses of epic struggles with heavy trains. On that fearsome initial gradient of 1 in 50 the speed was usually below 20 mph on entering the first tunnel, and to go through that close bore on the second of two engines that were both going practically all out was a grisly experience, even to a hardened steam footplate rider. Physical conditions apart, the working of that line was a perennial headache when the traffic was at its maximum at summer week-ends. There was no signalbox in the four miles between Bath Junction and

Midford and because of the fearful gradients, it would take between nine and ten minutes to get through. Motorists of today are all too well aware of how frustrating and time consuming even a short section of single-line traffic can be on a highway, and then imagine what it could be like on a summer Saturday between Bath Junction and Midford. On a railway there is no chance of following, head to tail, once the green light has been given for a move. A second train cannot proceed until the first one has cleared the farther end; and that would mean waiting about ten minutes, while those regulating the movements would also have to consider the queue of trains building up to come through the opposite way!

Many, many years before I came to live near Bath I used to visit relatives in Harrogate. My uncle's business was then in Bradford, and each evening the family car used to meet him at Otley, to which he travelled by a Midland train, and avoided the need to go via Leeds and have to change. That daily road journey, if made today, could well be a pilgrimage over abandoned railways. Otley no longer has a railway, but the one-time layout can be readily traced on the one-inch Ordnance map. No fewer than three organisations were involved in this small area. The line to Ilkley is a busy modern route, and the one-time connections at the Menston and Burley junctions can be spotted if one can secure a front seat in one of the diesel multiple-unit trains running either from Leeds or Bradford. Approaching Ilkley the junction with the one-time very picturesque Midland line onwards to Skipton can be descried, which may be traced from the highways A65, B6160 and A59 in succession.

The line between Otley and Ilkley was jointly owned by the North Eastern and Midland companies, but the operation appears to have been far from joint. They competed for the considerable passenger traffic, and if the holder of a season ticket issued by one company dared to enter a carriage belonging to the other, he was likely to be summarily ejected by the staff at the next station. Eastwards from Otley the now-abandoned route was purely North Eastern and it ended in a triangle junction with the Leeds Northern mainline at Arthington. This long-dismantled junction has an historic interest in the beginnings of

Lines to Otley and Ilkley.

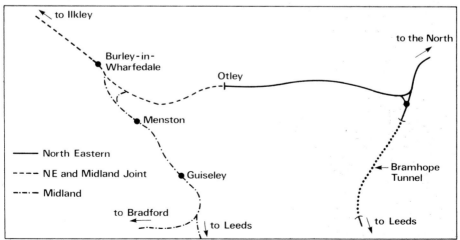

electric signalling, for it was at one of the prongs of the triangle that the points were operated by low voltage direct current supplied from batteries, rather than a mains electricity system.

Continuing north-eastwards towards Harrogate one soon comes within sight of a stupendous piece of railway architecture, the great viaduct of 31 arches, of a maximum height of 110 feet, spanning the broad valley of the Crimple Beck. Until one traces out the abandoned routes in this area the geography of the present line from Leeds to Harrogate does not make sense. But the fashionable spa town was at first approached by two separate and bitterly hostile railways. George Hudson's York and North Midland came up from the south-east on very steep gradients from Wetherby and it was this line that, emerging from Crimple Tunnel, built the magnificent viaduct across the valley to reach the high ground on which Harrogate itself is perched. The Leeds Northern, running north-east on the southern slopes of the valley made a broad sweep round the base of the hill, avoiding steep gradients, and made its Harrogate station on the eastern extremities of the town, at Starbeck. It was not until both one-time rival railways were merged into the North Eastern, in 1854, that connection between the two at Crimple Junction was made. Between the steep hillside and the southern end of the great viaduct there was not much space, and the linking line went round in a very sharp curve.

Times have indeed changed since that early link-up. In the days of the London and North Eastern Railway the route from Harrogate to Leeds via the Crimple junction and curve, and the old Leeds Northern, became part of a

The approaches to Harrogate.

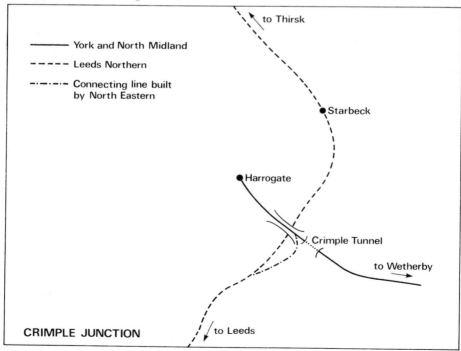

Crimple viaduct (Tomlinson's North Eastern Railway).

through Anglo-Scottish express route followed by no less a train than the *Queen of Scots* Pullman. At one time, however, prior to this routing, the LNER ran the Edinburgh Pullman non-stop between Harrogate and Kings Cross, using the former York and North Midland Line, taking the straight line at Crimple Junction, through the tunnel, and at high speed down the hill to Wetherby. Only the 'dog's hind leg' route, from the viaduct round to the Leeds Northern, remains, though the tracks of the old lines are clear enough on the ground, as is equally the portal of Crimple Tunnel—referred to as 'Prospect Tunnel' on the latest Ordnance maps.

Going north from Harrogate the next stop made by the *Queen of Scots* Pullman express used to be at Darlington, which is a good place from which to start on an exploration of that most appealing westward extension of the Stockton and Darlington, the one time South Durham and Lancashire Union Railway. But why Lancashire? Its western extremities made junctions with the Lancaster and Carlisle main line at Tebay, in Westmorland, and at Clifton (near Penrith) in Cumberland! It was at Tebay, however, that the significance of that old name could be discerned, because its staple traffic, admirably reciprocal, was coal and coke westbound, and iron ore eastbound with the western terminal point at Barrow-in-Furness. The line forked at Kirkby Stephen, whence the more northerly prong went on to Penrith, to give access to the Cockermouth, Keswick and Penrith Railway, which was a joint concern of the London and North Western, and of the North Eastern. I explored the line from that choicest of vantage points—the locomotive footplate—one gloriously fine mid-summer evening back in 1951. The line has been closed for some time and the track lifted, but its course, like so many others, can readily be traced on those bleak hillsides.

On that far off evening in 1951 we were not working a massive iron ore train from the Furness district, or anything like it, but a little three-coach, cross-country passenger train, hauled by a delightful little North Eastern goods engine of 1886 vintage. From Kirkby Stephen where, on the eastbound journey, the serious climbing began, the line toiled over the open hillside, far away from any roads, till one came to a shoulder of the fells, swung round in a south-easterly direction and saw, far ahead as yet, the incredibly light and almost fairylike structure of Belah viaduct. Now alas Belah is gone. When railways are closed, unless the material is needed locally and can be economically moved, the great masonry works are usually left *in situ*; but iron or steel is another matter. If left to decay, unpainted, it can become a great danger. Belah was a mighty structure in wrought iron, 1,040 feet long, with 16 spans of 60 feet and a total maximum height of 196 feet. Crossing it on the footplate of an engine was an awe-inspiring experience; but on that lovely calm evening I could not help wondering what it would be like in the teeth of a winter's gale!

Above Belah glen, with the line still climbing steeply, the railway draws near to the A66 highway, and eventually reaches Stainmore Summit, within a few feet of the highest-ever railway altitude in England, 1,370 feet above ordance datum. On that far off journey of mine it was then 9.30 pm and I was able to look back from this high altitude, and see the sun setting over the distant heights of Galloway, so marvellously clear was the visibility. Here, on this railway of high romance, one inevitably looked back to former years to the great mineral traffic of the time before the iron ore mines of the Furness district were worked out and when coal and coke from South Durham had to be hauled over the very rest of the Pennines to feed the blast furnaces at Conishead Priory, Barrow, Askam and Millom. Pause on the crest of the range between Barras and Bowes, and picture the big 0-8-0 freighters of the North Eastern coming up from their crossing of the Belah viaduct with their loads of iron ore.

The London and North Western Railway, though providing the line from Tebay, had no hand in this massive traffic. They had accorded running powers to the Furness Railway over the great Anglo-Scottish main line as far south as Hincaster Junction, and this brings us to another long-dismantled section of railway. Drawing near to the wide sandy estuary of the River Kent the one-time branch of the Furness Railway can be traced past Heversham to the village of Sandside, and so to the junction with the Furness main line at Arnside. On many of the older lines, and the Furness and its various constituents could be considered as one of them, passenger stations have been swept away wholesale; but not so in this intriguing area. As the train of today continues westward towards Barrow there is Plumpton Junction, just after crossing the Leven estuary—no longer a junction—but once the starting point of the branch to Conisland Priory and of the triangle junction with the line that led to Lakeside, Windermere. The eastern spur of the triangle at Plumpton had some vicissitudes. The track was taken up in the First World War to provide material for wartime railways; it was relaid afterwards, but removed again when the whole branch was considered no longer viable.

As one draws nearer to Barrow there are innumerable lines leading to worked out iron ore mines. Even when my father's business was in the district, some 65 years ago, many of these mineral lines had fallen into disuse, though the tracks remained, overgrown with grass. Easily the most interesting of the old lines in the neighbourhood of Barrow was the branch to Piel, over which there was a service of four passenger trains a day (seven on Saturday) until the First World War. Piel Pier, on Roa Island, was the first terminus of the Furness Railway. It was reached over a causeway across the Rampside Sands, owned by a certain

Opposite page top *Belah viaduct* (Ian S. Pearsall). **Centre** *Bela viaduct, on the Furness branch line from Arnside to Hincaster junction—a photograph taken in the last years of its service* (Ian S. Pearsall). **Bottom** *Greenodd station, on the now closed Furness Railway branch line from Plumpton Junction to Windermere, lakeside.*

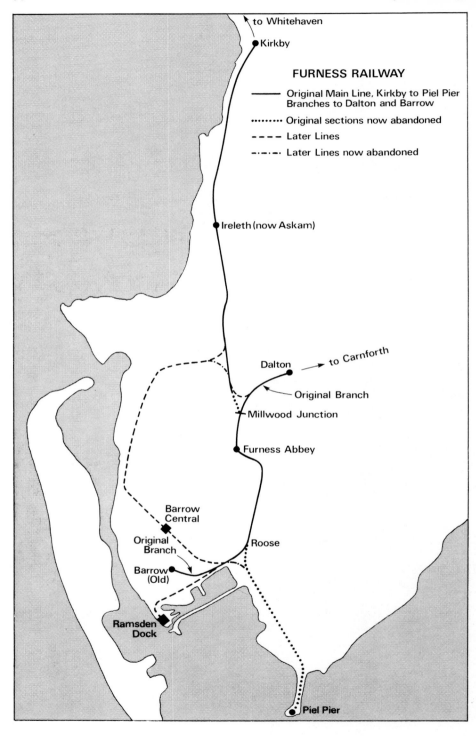

to Whitehaven

● Kirkby

FURNESS RAILWAY

——— Original Main Line, Kirkby to Piel Pier
         Branches to Dalton and Barrow

·········· Original sections now abandoned

– – – – Later Lines

–·–·– Later Lines now abandoned

● Ireleth (now Askam)

Dalton ——→ to Carnforth
●

Original Branch

⊢ Millwood Junction

● Furness Abbey

◆ Barrow
   Central

Original
Branch

Barrow ●
(Old)

Roose
●

◆ Ramsden
   Dock

⊙ ● Piel Pier

Opposite *The Barrow line to Piel Pier.* **Above** *Roa Island station, Furness Railway.*

John Abel Smith, who ran a steamboat service across Morecambe Bay, to Fleetwood. As a boy, barely into my 'teens' I remember cycling out across that causeway to Roa Island and seeing the rusting tracks of the disused railway, though even before that time the direct connecting line from the north that constituted the original main line had been removed. In Barrow itself there was a line that led down to a station adjacent to Ramsden Dock, from which, prior to the First World War, there was a nightly steamer service to Belfast. The evening train from Carnforth, was specially labelled *Belfast Boat Express* and had connections from London, Leeds and Manchester.

Although I happen to know the Furness district intimately it does provide an excellent example of how one can dig into past railway history, with the aid of large scale maps and a study of old timetables, all of which are preserved in museums and reference libraries dealing particularly with transport. But in the Furness district there is also scope for a truly spectacular 'dig' in the true archaeological style because, on October 22 1892, a subsidence beneath the main line sidings at Lindal Moor and the formation of a large hole at the surface at about 8.15 am led to one of the standard 0-6-0 goods engines sinking into the cavity. The driver and firemen jumped clear, and although the subsidence was gradual and breakdown tackle was quickly obtained, the engine could not be saved. Four hours later it had completely disappeared. It is estimated that its

The now abandoned station, Broughton-in-Furness.

remains are now some 200 feet below the surface—but what an opportunity for a dig!

Another very interesting field of study for abandoned and largely vanished routes is the area immediately north and south of the Solway Firth. Even in the earliest days of railways in the Border country, Carlisle was a point of traffic congestion, as could well be imagined from the number of lines feeding into the one through route. When, in the early 1860s, a potentially good traffic began to develop in iron ore from the mines of West Cumberland to the blast furnaces of Lanarkshire, a new line, known as the Solway Junction Railway, was incorporated under an Act of Parliament in June 1864 to by-pass the entire Carlisle complex. It was no mere local deviation. It began at Kirtlebridge, on the Caledonian main line, some eight miles north-west of Gretna, and went south, crossing the Glasgow and South Western main line at Annan, and then striking out clean across the Solway Firth on a viaduct second only in length, on the British railways, to the Forth Bridge! It was 1,940 yards long, built entirely in cast iron, with 181 single piers and 12 double piers. There was no question of providing clearance beneath it for navigation and, even at low tide, the rail level was only about 35 feet above the water.

On the English side the line continued south to a trailing junction with a branch of another Scottish railway, the North British, which had a line from

The Solway Junction Railway and its connections showing the lines and their original ownership.

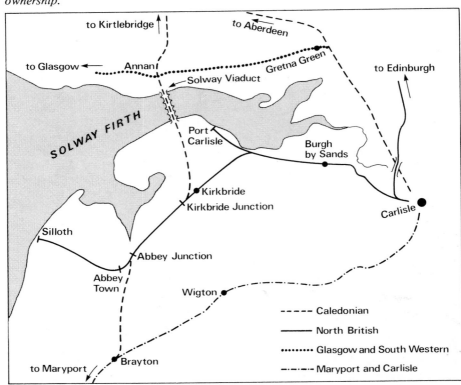

Carlisle to Silloth. This north to south by-pass then continued, by exercise of running powers, for $3\frac{3}{4}$ miles on the North British, from Kirkbride Junction to Abbey Junction, at which latter point it turned due south again, on its own metals, to join the main line of the Maryport and Carlisle Railway, at Brayton. The total length was $21\frac{1}{4}$ miles and almost from the outset it was worked by the Caledonian; but with the decline of the ore traffic its usefulness and viability ceased, and the closing of the line during the First World War really marked the beginning of the end. Although it was re-opened again in 1920 the service south of Annan was withdrawn a year later, when it was considered that the long viaduct was no longer safe. I may add that, after the termination of the railway service across the viaduct, it began to partake of a new, though quite illicit function. The citizens of Annan used it as a footbridge to gain access to English soil on a Sunday; and in Bowness-on-Solway to get a drink that was then denied to them in their own country!

Proceeding farther north, the railway archaeology of the City of Glasgow would provide material for whole books, let alone a passing mention in a single chapter. I have before me the extraordinarily complex network of lines depicted on the Railway Clearing House map of 1897 and, comparing this with a large scale map of the city as it is today, one is amazed at the number of terminal stations that then existed, quite apart from the relatively recent eliminations of the major passenger stations of St Enoch and Buchanan Street. Places such as Bridge Street, General Terminus, South Side, used for main line passenger trains before the the River Clyde was bridged in the heart of the city, and the Glasgow and South Western principal goods station, College, stir the imagination. The access to College, on the map, looks like one of those strangely inconvenient layouts of goods stations in the City of London, or rather worse. To get a goods train into or out of the terminus it would have to be drawn out along a line owned by the North British. It was no minor line either, leading into Queen Street low level station. I have arrived in Glasgow on a main line express from Newcastle round the curve at Bellgrove, and into the low level part of Queen Street, when the high level terminus was congested with week-end traffic.

Up in the Highlands, a line now abandoned by British Railways, is the section of the original Highland main line between Aviemore and Forres. The northern end of this, between Aviemore and Grantown-on-Spey is being preserved and operated by the 'Strathspey Railway' but the more interesting part (from the engineering and operating viewpoint) is now closed. The authorisation of the Highland Railway was a highly contentious business. Rival interests at first ridiculed the idea of taking a railway over the Grampian Mountains at an altitude of 1,484 feet in the Pass of Druimuachdar; but in Inverness opinion was solidly behind the proposal and, with a mixture of tact and cunning, they advanced their first line along the coast of the Moray Firth, from Nairn to Forres, thereby constituting an effective block towards the aspirations of those who would reach Inverness from Aberdeen, and make that the principal way to the south. Fortunately for the Inverness interests, the proceedings of the Aberdeen party spent themselves in speech-making and threats rather than actual achievement, and when the Invernessians tried again and, in 1861, submitted a Bill for an Inverness and Perth Junction Railway, from Forres to the south, they were successful.

From the moment of striking south from Forres the single-tracked line was on

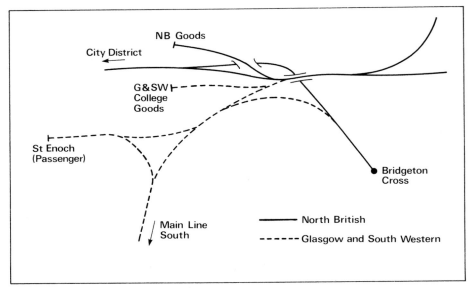

Glasgow, College goods, and its access lines.

heavy gradients and, although at first following roughly the course of the River Findhorn, the distinguished engineer, Joseph Mitchell, a native of Inverness, had to resort to numerous twists and turns to maintain an even rising gradient of 1 in 75. The track can be traced from roads adjacent, where it mounts into the beautiful Altyre Woods and the A940 highway draws alongside the railway at Dunphail station. Just beyond here is the most spectacular engineering work on the line, the graceful seven-arched viaduct, in granite, over the river Divie. Beyond this the line, continuing to climb on a gradient of 1 in 70, mounts high above the tree line to some of the bleakest and most inhospitable regions traversed by any main line railway in Great Britain. The Ordnance Survey maps pinpoint much of the area as 'rough pasture': rough indeed, also, for the trains! At an altitude of about 1,000 feet above sea level the line across the dreaded Dava Moor is completely exposed to every wind under Heaven, and the stories of winter snow-blocks up there are now legendary. On the A939 highway from Dava station—or what is left of it—southwards towards Grantown-on-Spey, one can drive within sight of, or immediately beside, the line and, even on the fairest day, it does not need a great deal of imagination to picture what things could be like when the snow fiend really gets going up on Dava Moor.

One could see the lines of snow fences set some 50 yards back from the railway, pallisades built up of old sleepers, burnt in places during the summer by sparks thrown out from hard worked locomotives. Then, no less significant, were the tall posts for carrying the signal wires. Normally these were quite short and carried the wires at no more than a few inches above track level; but on the more exposed parts of the Highland Railway the posts were a good six feet tall and carried the wires well about the level of a normal snowfall. To delve more into the history and construction of the line I would recommend a study of a paper read by the engineer himself, Joseph Mitchell, to a meeting of the British Association at Dundee, in September 1867.

Chapter 5

Changed station layouts

To the railway historian there is perhaps nothing so fascinating as the tracing out of old station layouts, though from the viewpoint of pure archaeology it can be frustrating. Although there was nothing parsimonious or parochial about the pioneers of the British railway system, even those great seers would hardly have imagined how traffic developed in the latter part of the 19th century, causing the majestic terminal stations they planned to be substantially enlarged. The trouble has been that successive enlargements have swept away relics of the earlier layouts. In the interests of improved railway operating this is understandable, but it means that one's research into the past has to be done with the aid of old documents, maps and such like, rather than by exploration on the ground. Even so, it can be an enthralling study. Of this there is no more striking example than that of Euston.

No longer ago than 1960 the great old station was a railway archaeologist's paradise. The simple 'train shed' built by Robert Stephenson in 1837 was still there, including the old columns and the beautiful cast iron spandrels supporting the roof. That roof was designed by Charles Fox, one of those amazing young men of pioneer railway days who were ready to 'have a go' at anything. Long before he embarked on his career in architecture, which in due course brought him a knighthood, he had worked for one of Stephenson's rivals and had, in fact, driven the *Novelty* for John Ericsson at the Rainhill trials in 1829. Thereafter, for a time, he was a regular driver on the Liverpool and Manchester Railway. Two contemporary illustrations between them convey the elegance of the original layout at Euston, and the neatness and simplicity of the traffic operation, at the time when the trains were hauled up Camden bank by cable. The beautiful Ackerman coloured print, famed for depicting so vividly as much the costumes of the passengers as the design of the early rolling stock, shows more subtly the architecture of what was termed 'the departure stage' of the station, and the neat arrangement of the retaining walls in the yard, and the fine arches of the Wriothesley Street bridge, at the end of the station yard.

The ground plan of the station, as included in Simms' *Public Works of Great Britain*, published in 1838, is extremely revealing in the way it shows instantly that the London and Birmingham Railway at the very outset were planning for an enlargement and development of their business. Camden bank, for example, was laid with four tracks, the 1 in 70 incline beginning immediately beneath the Wriothesley Street bridge. It seems evident that a duplication of the track facilities to the west of the main carriage drive was envisaged from the extent of

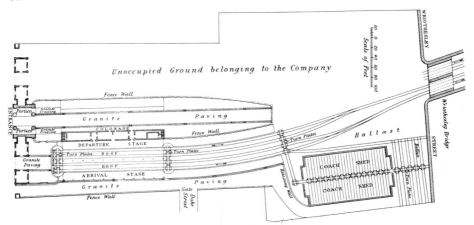

Above *Euston Station in 1837.* **Opposite page top** *'The Station at Euston Square' from one of the Ackermann prints.* **Centre** *Euston: arrival platforms circa 1890, showing (to left) the columns and arches of the original station.* **Bottom** *Euston: No 6 departure platform (the original departure platform of the first station) with the 2 pm Scotch 'Corridor' train ready to leave.*

the original purchase of the land. All the coaching stock was four-wheeled and facilities for transfer from one track to another, or into and out of the coach shed, was made by means of turntables and human push-power. How old Euston grew into the vast agglomeration of tracks and platforms that existed in 1960 can be traced from successive maps; but it may be a point of some significance that up till 1916 its most famous train, the 2 pm Anglo-Scottish corridor dining car express—the 'Corridor', as it was always known in the service—left from the original 'departure stage' of 1837, No 6 platform in later years, rather than from one of the long new platforms 13, 14 or 15 on the west side of the station. As a boy of 11 years old I travelled by that train in 1916.

In 1846 Euston became much more than the terminus of the London and Birmingham Railway, for in that year the company amalgamated with the Grand Junction to form the London and North Western, at once and for three quarters of a century, Britain's 'Premier Line'. Extensions had already begun on the unoccupied ground to the west and a challenge was already arising to Euston's position as the original, and one-time only, gateway from London to the north. The wrangles, thrusts and counterthrusts towards a direct line from London to York were in full blast, and the far-seeing men of the LNWR sought to consolidate and strengthen their position before any rival should appear on the scene. So, at what would be the mid-point of their enlarged station—immediately behind the Doric Arch—they built the utterly magnificent Great Hall. In this chapter I am concerned mainly with tracks. The grand edifices of the past are dealt with later. But to the west of where the Great Hall was built, new platforms for main line traffic were added, together with some additional short ones, in the 'vee' between the original layout and the new one.

The roofing over the new west platforms was designed in the same style as that of Charles Fox's original and formed a companion piece to the west of the Great Hall. What eventually became No 9 platform was, at one time, among the

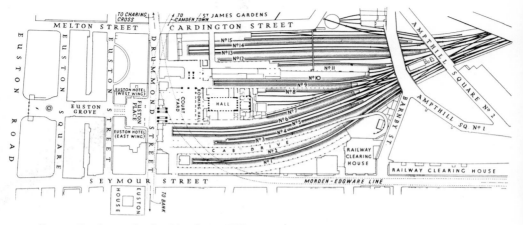

Euston Station as finalised by the LNWR.

most important in the station. In that 'vee', between platforms 6 and 9, however, there was a piece of history. When plans were in hand for the resignalling of the station in 1951 and Westinghouse secured the contract, I was intrigued, in studying track plans, to find one connection leading into a short platform not accessible to the public named 'Irish Mail Line'. At first I wondered exceedingly. Between the two World Wars when I had known Euston intimately the Irish Mails, both night and day, were long and heavy trains and could not possibly have been accommodated on that short line. Furthermore, the night mail, which left at 8.45 pm, was the centre of a picturesque tradition that dated back even beyond the days of stage coaches, indeed to the galloping post-boys. Each night the 'King's Time' used to be sent from London to Dublin, in the form of a watch brought by special messenger from the General Post Office in St Martins-le-Grand, and handed to the postmaster of the mail train, who would in turn hand it to the captain of the packet steamer at Holyhead.

But things were not always so peaceful between Great Britain and Ireland as they became after the treaty of 1922. In the Victorian era feeling ran very high at times, and there was more than one threat to dynamite the Irish Mail, by which vital dispatches between London and Dublin were carried. One could not run the risk of loading such 'freight', or indeed any mail, into the travelling post office carriages on a platform open to the general public; and so the mail portion of the train was loaded in a secluded siding occult from public gaze from which the locomotive would draw the vans at the last minute and back them on to the public part of the train ready to start away on time. Although its use for its original purpose had long since ceased, the name 'Irish Mail Line' remained on the track plans of Euston until the great modernisation for electric traction began in 1963. How every vestige of the old station was swept away in subsequent years, including those two architectural masterpieces, the Doric Arch and the Great Hall, is referred to in more detail in the next chapter. It is, however, sometimes not only in trying to trace out history, but in severely practical matters, that lack of old plans can prove a major headache.

At the outer ends of the old platforms, numbered 3 to 9, where there was a positive maze of intersecting lines, the whole area was bricked over, making

Euston: outer end, east side, with tracks bricked in.

one huge 'level crossing' over which men could walk, with wheel barrows and so on, without the necessity of stepping over rails. The upkeep of this vast area of bricks must have been considerable, and when it began to fall into disrepair in the First World War it was removed and never replaced. In the changed conditions of working its going was no disadvantage. In the lean years of the 1930s, however, another economy measure had some repercussions at the time of the first resignalling, in 1951-2. My colleagues who were responsible for installing the new electro-pneumatic point gear found that the 'permanent way' was not very permanent in many places. In wet weather the ballasting became waterlogged with clay working up, enabling the sleepers to move about. It was then revealed that there were no plans in existence of the drainage system. In the 1930s, as an economy measure, the old 'drains gang' had been disbanded, and its work transferred elsewhere. The foreman, on being made redundant, destroyed all the plans!

For those seeking to unearth the history of terminal stations, Waterloo provides no less fruitful a field than Euston. The only thing is that the process of evolution from first opening to the station of today took place in much shorter time: 1848 to 1922, against 1837 to 1966 at Euston. In Victorian times Waterloo grew up in much the same piecemeal fashion, except that it had a rapidly growing suburban traffic which Euston did not have to contend with. The intensity of passenger working in the morning and evening rush hours compelled the introduction of the most advanced safety signalling appliances in every succeeding era and, except in one remarkably picturesque association, the development at Waterloo is closely linked with that of signalling itself. Unlike Euston, however, Waterloo was not the first choice for the terminus of the London and Southampton Railway. This was at first located at Nine Elms, later to be the site of the locomotive works, and still later the goods terminal. But when eastward extension from Nine Elms was projected, the London and South Western Railway, as it had become, sought connection with the railways running east and south-east from London.

There was a proposal to build a connecting line eastwards from 'Waterloo Bridge', as the new station was at first known, to link up with the Croydon and

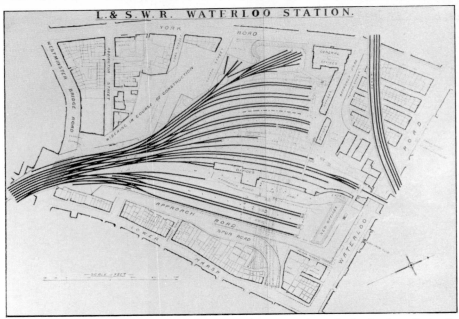

Waterloo: the old station with single track connection, through the back wall, to the South Eastern Railway.

the Greenwich lines at London Bridge. This was before the South Eastern had come westward from London Bridge. But this proposal, for which authority had been obtained, was allowed to lapse through lack of money. Then, however, in 1859, a line called the London Bridge and Charing Cross was authorised. This also languished for a time; but, when the South Eastern took it over, in 1863, and went ahead with the work, the London and South Western saw an easy way of getting to London Bridge, since the new line would pass 'through their back garden' as it were. So they made a single track connection, across the concourse of their terminal building at Waterloo, through the back wall and over a bridge to a junction with the South Eastern Railway. From Waterloo Junction, as the point of connection was named, the South Western obtained running powers to London Bridge. Having built this connecting link and secured the authority, the South Western never ran a service of their own over it.

Waterloo: the old station circa 1900.

Charing Cross, South Eastern Railway, 1864 (The Museum of British Railways, Clapham).

The link was used in some rather curious ways. The only regular passenger service was operated by the London and *North* Western, of all railways! They ran a 'round London' service from Euston via Willesden, the West London line, and Waterloo, terminating at London Bridge. It would have been a real connoisseur's trip, for the ride, but not for any practical purposes! The London and South Western, however, had a very good reason for maintaining that link in first class condition. In Victorian times the Queen came to use the LSWR from Windsor for her journeys to the Continent, and then the Royal Train travelled via Waterloo, over the connecting bridge to the South Eastern, and thence to Dover. It was used also for the special trains of visiting royalty, en route for Windsor. The connecting line ran between the platform tracks of Nos 4 and 5 platforms, and at the buffer-stops end there was an opening bridge providing a walkway between Nos 4 and 5. Beyond this bridge the concourse was sloped down to track level to facilitate crossing by barrows and such like. Fortunately this phase in the evolution of Waterloo is well documented by drawings and photographs, though no one ever seems to have photographed a train crossing the concourse.

Charing Cross station was opened in 1864, and quite recently there was a sensational 'find' of some huge glass plate negatives that must have been taken soon after that opening. They show a wealth of fascinating detail in track-work, signals, locomotives, some gorgeously ornate lamps and, not least, the original station roof. This was a handsome arched structure that became a prominent feature of Victorian London. Forty-one years later, in December 1905, part of it collapsed, in circumstances that constituted the luckiest escape from one of the most terrible catastrophes that could have afflicted the railways of Great Britain. By the greatest of good fortune it occurred at a quiet period in mid-afternoon, and the only casualties were three workmen. A tie-rod in one of the roof trusses broke, owing to a flaw in welding during the original manufacture. The flaw was internal, and could not have been detected save by X-ray

Above *Charing Cross, about 1870, showing SER locomotives and early signals.* **Below** *Charing Cross: looking out across the river bridge showing the first signal box and signals.*

photography. During the life of the roof the flaw had gradually opened out until it finally caused the rod to break altogether. What could have happened if the rod had lasted another two hours, and the roof had crashed when the station was crowded with home-going commuters, does not bear thinking about.

At the seaward end of the South Eastern Railway, at Dover, the process of railway evolution since the establishment of the first terminus station there, in 1844, provides material for an absorbing study. The background, over a period of 70 years, is often one of naval strategy but equally that of 'cat and dog' railway politics, rather than archaeology. But while in the close and efficient integration of modern facilities few traces remain of Victorian days, the archives of the Dover Harbour Board, and the records of the municipal authorities contain a wealth of material to delight the researcher, and which enabled me, in one of my earlier books, to build up a reasonably clear picture of conditions at several critical stages in the development. When the South Eastern Railway first arrived at Dover, in 1844, the Admiralty Pier did not exist, and the terminus station, Dover Town, was built on the seashore as near as was convenient to the primitive quay from which the packets sailed to Calais and Ostend. As construction (begun in 1847) proceeded, a single track line was taken across the cobblestones on to the pier. This latter was built wide enough to take two tracks abreast, and when the London, Chatham and Dover Railway arrived, and likewise extended from its Dover Harbour station, the tracks of the deadly rivals ran alongside, but in no way connected. A memorable water colour painting by Howard Geach vividly portrays the conditions in which passengers of the 1860s changed from boat to train at Dover.

The names of the ordinary passenger stations in Dover were not really appropriate, because neither the 'Town', of the South Eastern, nor the

Dover: the Admiralty Pier with paddle steamers berthed on both sides.

'Harbour' of the London Chatham and Dover were conveniently sited. Of course the geographical situation made things difficult, with the range of white cliffs so close to the shore, and the boat trains of both companies ran through the ordinary stations without stopping. Even after the Chatham and South Eastern companies had been brought together in a working alliance under a common Managing Committee, in 1898, the complicated track configurations at Dover remained, except that connecting lines were laid in between the two, on the immediate approach to the Admiralty Pier, and elsewhere. But a new complication had been introduced by the Dover Harbour Board building a new commercial pier of their own, the Prince of Wales, to which railway connection was made, with the intention of using it as a relief to the facilities available on the Admiralty Pier, and for occasional use by ocean-going liners. But the railway connection to it was very slow, and roundabout, over sharp curves, and along an open quay side to reach a narrow pier. For ordinary packet services it was just 'not on', to use a modern colloquialism.

The enterprise that lifted the whole situation of marine traffic at Dover from its historic complications to a truly splendid modern concept was that of the South Eastern and Chatham Managing Committee in building the Marine Station, on which work began in 1910. The reclaiming of a large area of the inner part of the harbour, to accommodate the extensive track, platform and station building facilities, imposed a new situation upon the working of the Continental traffic meanwhile. The steamer berths nearest to the shore could no longer be used, and the boat trains had to be taken right out on to the Admiralty Pier extension, beyond the old lighthouse. The transition between the original and the extended part of the pier involved quite a sharp curve past the fort and the lighthouse, and one boyhood recollection, of a visit to Dover in 1911, remains clearly in mind. With my parents I walked down to the far end of the pier extension, and we were there when the 2.20 pm Ostend Boat Express arrived. I remember how shocked I was at the speed it came round those curves by the lighthouse, and the way the engine heeled over! As always on the Admiralty Pier the change from train to boat was made completely in the open,

Dover: aerial view after construction of the new Marine Station (top right), but showing also the 'Prince of Wales' pier (left) and connecting railway.

sometimes with the sea breaking clean over the breakwater. In winter storms coaches were sometimes overturned with the force of a wave crashing over them. Those were the days!

Another area where I have personally seen the whole configuration of railways change, and many old landmarks swept away, is around Leeds and Bradford. When I first began to travel in the area, from 1916 onwards, there were five major railways working into Leeds. There were the three great Anglo-Scottish protagonists from London, the Great Northern, Midland, and London and North Western, plus the North Eastern and the Lancashire and Yorkshire. Those five worked into three stations, all in the heart of the city, but it was not always so. The Leeds and Selby Railway, completed in 1834, was the first, and its terminus was at Marsh Lane, three-quarters of a mile east of the present City station. It was approached by a tunnel, 700 yards long under Richmond Hill, which had some very handsome masonry façades. Little amenities for passengers were deemed necessary. There were no platforms and no waiting rooms, and travellers waiting for the trains were kept under the entrance portico, or the station shed. After the Leeds and Selby Railway had become part of the North Eastern in 1854, and the Marsh Lane terminus had become the railhead for an increasingly extensive group of lines to the east, proposals were made to extend the line westwards to a more appropriate station in the city itself, instead of on the outskirts; but the first scheme encountered such opposition from the citizens of Leeds that it was dropped. It was not until 1869 that the large 'New' station was opened, to be jointly owned with the London and North Western.

The first trunk line to come into Leeds was the North Midland, so splendidly engineered by George Stephenson, and opened throughout between Leeds and Derby in May 1840. It is curious, however, that although he always envisaged a network of railways covering the whole of Great Britain, Stephenson led his lines into what were virtually dead ends in so many large towns, with no ready means of continuation or interlinking with others. The eastern end of the Liverpool and Manchester Railway was built as a terminus, and it had to be by-passed when the line was continued eastward. It was the same at Leeds, where

Birmingham, New Street, as first opened in 1854.

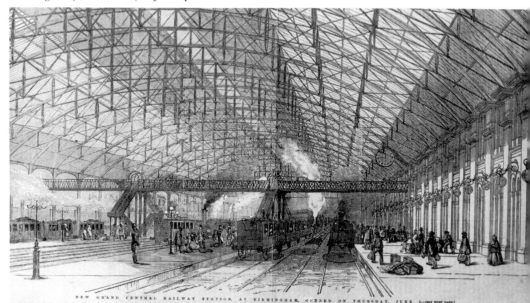

the original terminus was at Hunslet Lane, about half a mile south of the city centre. Wellington station, which became the Midland Railway headquarters in Leeds, was the terminus of the Leeds and Bradford Railway, and was opened in 1846. It was convenient for the business centre, surrounding City Square, but was inconvenient from the railway operating point of view, involving a reversal of direction for trains proceeding beyond Leeds. It must be admitted that, in the Paget era, from 1907 onwards, the operating was extremely 'slick' at Wellington station with the Scotch Expresses—so much so that on at least one recorded occasion the station stop, despite reversal of direction, was so brief that one of the porters from the adjoining Queens Hotel had an unexpected trip to Carlisle. The train started while he was still stowing some passengers' luggage on the racks of a first class compartment!

The Leeds, Dewsbury and Manchester was the next line to arrive, from the south-west and opening the Central Station in 1848. This latter station, less than ten minutes walk from the Midland, equally had no pretence to architectural distinction. The original company became part of the London and North Western but, curiously enough, although that company retained a part share in the ownership, in later years it ran no passenger trains into the station, for reasons to be mentioned later. In 1849 the Leeds and Thirsk, later the Leeds Northern, made Central their terminus, coming in alongside the Leeds and Bradford line of the Midland near Armley, and then curving round to join the North Western at Holbeck. The situation of the Lancashire and Yorkshire Railway at Leeds was always a case of 'by your leave'. One of its principal constituents was the Manchester and Leeds Railway, which never reached Leeds on its own tracks. It made a trailing junction with the Midland at Goose Hill Junction, near Normanton, and exercised running powers from there first to Hunslet Lane, and then into Wellington.

Then into the already crowded railway arena of the West Riding of Yorkshire

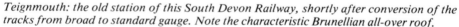

Teignmouth: the old station of this South Devon Railway, shortly after conversion of the tracks from broad to standard gauge. Note the characteristic Brunellian all-over roof.

came the Great Northern—at first, equally 'by your leave', over Lancashire and Yorkshire tracks as far as Methley, seven miles short of Leeds, and wonderful to relate, over the Midland! In view of the stop-at-nothing tactics George Hudson had employed to try and prevent the Great Northern getting its Act of Incorporation, it is surprising that this concession was ever granted; but it was an uneasy arrangement and did not last long. In 1854 the Great Northern enterprised a line of its own from Bradford to Leeds, entering the Exchange station of the L & YR at the former town, and the Central at Leeds. This move was also to the advantage of the Lancashire and Yorkshire, which as a *quid pro quo* obtained running powers over the Great Northern line into Leeds Central. Thereafter, through Halifax and Low Moor, they had a line from Manchester that was independent of the Midland. The Great Northern itself cast off the Midland incubus in 1857 by building a line of its own from Wakefield to join its Leeds and Bradford line at the Wortley triangle, and with four companies using Central station, arrangements were made for joint ownership of the last 25 chains of track, and of the station itself, from the oddly named 'Three Signal Bridge Junction'. The ownership thence forward was Great Northern, Lancashire and Yorkshire, London and North Western and North Eastern Joint—the North Eastern having absorbed the Leeds Northern. The accommodation was by no means commodious, and one can imagine operation was at times a bit chaotic.

After the establishment of the North Eastern Railway in 1854 the situation for the development of that large company's business in Leeds was not satisfactory, with the former Leeds Northern funnelling into the crowded confines of Central, and the line from Selby and the east ending at Marsh Lane. Furthermore there was a desire to link up with the London and North Western in running through cross-country services from Newcastle, and the North East ports, via Leeds, to Huddersfield, Manchester and Liverpool. So the great project of the large

Reading: the extraordinary single-platform station designed by Brunel, with the complicated track-work giving access to the one long platform.

'New' station was developed, to be situated alongside Wellington, for easy passenger interchange with the Midland. The completion of this station in 1869, and its connecting lines, changed the entire railway strategy of Leeds so far as the North Eastern and the London and North Western were concerned. Trains from the Leeds Northern crossed over on to Midland tracks at Wortley Junction, and then into the L & NW and NE Joint area at Canal Junction. The North Western put in a curve from Copley Hill Junction to Whitehall Junction to gain similar access; but at a later date the direct line from Farnley North Junction, entirely on arches, was built, giving an access that was independent of the Midland. So, Central was left to the Great Northern and the Lancashire and Yorkshire, with the North Western and the North Eastern free to develop their expanding traffics in the spacious 'New' station. This situation prevailed until after the railways of Britain were nationalised in 1948 when Central was closed, and everything concentrated in a rationalisation of facilities at Wellington and 'New'.

Perusal of family archives resulted in a 'dig' of a different kind concerning Bradford, a 'might-have-been', as distinct from a 'has been'. In his famous work, *The Rise and Progress of the Midland Railway*, F.S. Williams stated that in Bradford the company booked more travellers than on any other station on this system and, writing in the latter part of the 19th century, added '. . . it is arranging to provide four times the accommodation it now possesses'. This was at Forster Square station, most inconveniently located as a terminus at the end of what had originally been the Leeds and Bradford Railway but became, in the 1890s, a short branch from the main line to the North, from the triangle junction of Shipley. The great scheme of the 1890s was not only to provide more accommodation at Forster Square but to put Bradford on the main line to Scotland. An Act of 1898 authorised construction of a new line from Royston Junction via Thornhill, and in the approach to the city to dive clean underneath, and come out at Forster Square. The Midland excelled in its provision of alternative routes. Going north one could travel either via Leicester or Nottingham, or farther north one could go via Sheffield, or by George Stephenson's North Midland line. It would have been the same at Bradford. One could have taken the original route through Leeds, or by the new route from Royston Junction, north westwards via Thornhill, and then through Bradford. It would have put that most profitable of Midland passenger stations on the main line from London to Scotland.

The Midland Railway was, however, somewhat tardy in taking up the powers granted to them by the Act of 1898. Under the severely practical and rationalistic management of Guy Granet every means was sought of saving money and reducing passenger train mileage. Although the first link in the new line, from Royston Junction to Thornhill was completed and opened to traffic in 1906, and direct access to Bradford obtained by running powers over the Lancashire and Yorkshire line from Thornhill into Exchange terminus, an Abandonment Bill for the rest of the scheme was lodged with Parliament early in 1907. At once Bradford was in a state of turmoil. In the game of 'one-upmanship' which the city constantly played against its larger neighbour, Leeds, this was to have been a trump card. The main line to the north would have been six miles shorter, and the vexation of reversal of direction would have been avoided. Henceforth it would have been Leeds, and not Bradford, that would be out on a limb. An uncle of mine was then Town Clerk and, from the records

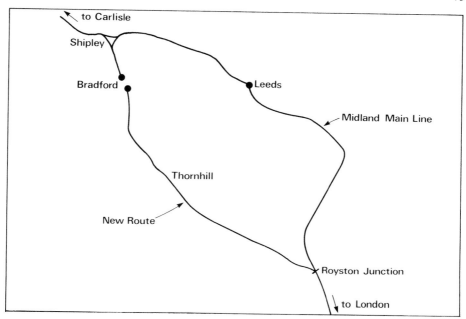

Above *Access to Bradford.*

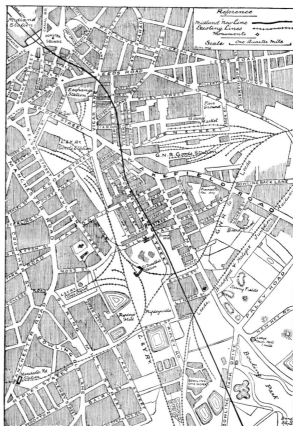

Right *Bradford: map from the* Yorkshire Daily Observer *showing the proposed direct line, in 1907, which would have put Bradford on the main line to Scotland.*

of his that I inherited, I found that the most urgent representations were made to the Midland Railway to reverse their decision to abandon. The critical point, on which the case for abandonment had been mainly based, was a guarantee that the Corporation had insisted upon (at the time of the 1898 Bill) safeguarding the integrity of certain water supplies which it was feared might be affected by the tunnelling under the city.

The Midland Railway now argued, in 1906, that the cost of meeting these guarantees would be so heavy as to make the proposed main line unacceptable; but opinion in Bradford was such, and the water supply so improved from what it had been in 1898, that the Corporation was prepared to relieve the Midland Railway of all responsibility in this respect. At a meeting in Derby in the first weeks of 1907 at which the Mayor of Bradford, and my uncle, together with two other members of the City Council, met Sir Ernest Paget, chairman of the MR, Guy Granet and Mr Beale, the railway company agreed to go ahead with the scheme. The usually well-informed *Yorkshire Daily Observer* of Saturday, February 16 1907, in an article beneath banner headlines, and occupying almost a whole page of the newspaper, published a map of the route the new line would take (see page 75). Sadly, however, after all this burst of activity, the proposal languished once again, and was never subsequently revived. After the Grouping of 1923, when the Midland and the Lancashire and Yorkshire came together in the LMS, the line from Royston to Thornhill was used for a new express service from Bradford to London, named *The Yorkshireman*, which ran from Exchange station over the former L & Y line to Thornhill; but, of course, this had no connections north of Bradford.

Chapter 6

Vanished edifices

A monument that became very familiar to travellers to and from Ireland, and seemed very much part of the railway scene, was the triumphal arch on the Admiralty Pier at Holyhead. Until 1920 the Irish Mail had been conveyed first by Admiralty sailing packets and then by the express steamers of the City of Dublin Steam Packet Company, and transfer of both mails and passengers took place on the exposed Admiralty Pier. The tracks on which the prestigious 'Irish Mail' ran made a detour round the memorial arch. Actually, although so very much associated with the running of the Irish Mail train, it dated back to 1821 when George IV paid a visit to Ireland. At his suggestion the fine harbour at Dun Laoghaire on the Irish side was renamed Kingstown, and on returning to Great Britain he ceremonially opened the arch on the Admiralty Pier at Holyhead. In 1920, however, the London and North Western Railway at last secured the Government contract for the seaward conveyance of the Irish Mail, and thereafter transference of mail and passengers from train to steamer took place at the inner harbour station, and the Admiralty Pier was abandoned.

Writing in the early months of 1980, with the British railway world agog with preparations for the 150th anniversary of the first-ever Inter-City railway, the Liverpool and Manchester, one cannot fail to be deeply impressed by the way the early railway pioneers sought to embellish their work. In connection with the

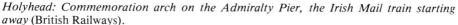

Holyhead: Commemoration arch on the Admiralty Pier, the Irish Mail train starting away (British Railways).

Liverpool and Manchester Railway one thinks instinctively of George Stephenson, of Chat Moss, the Rainhill locomotive trials, and sadly enough also of the first fatal railway accident in which W. Huskinsson was run over and killed on the opening day. But, although Stephenson and his band of eager young assistants were concerned with the basic hardware of the railway, working on a tight budget, the directors sought also the assistance of an architect. The railway, divined as an epochal event in the progress of the Industrial Revolution, and indeed in the social history of the British people, must have an appropriately grand point of entry. With discernment in respect of the degrees of enthusiasm towards the enterprise at opposite ends of the line— its general welcome in Liverpool against much hostility in Manchester—the directors commissioned a Liverpool man, John Foster, to produce a suitable design, for Liverpool. From the high ground east of the city, at Edge Hill, the line had to be carried steeply down, in tunnel, to the loading dock, and it was in the deep cutting leading to the tunnels that the excavation was made wide enough to accommodate four tracks. There, turntables were laid in, because it was at that point that locomotive haulage was to give place to cables, on the steep descending gradients through the tunnels. There also, at the eastward end of the excavation, John Foster's entrance arch to the main line to Manchester was built—the stupendous Moorish Arch.

I always feel that insufficient significance has been given to the symbolism of this remarkable edifice. It stands portentiously dominating the scene in contemporary drawings of the celebrated opening day in 1830 and, in its more functional aspect, it graces several of the famous Ackermann prints. But, when the original passenger station at Crown Street was superseded by the larger and more commodious Lime Street, the Moorish Arch was left in a backwater, as it were, to be demolished almost without notice in the very un-sentimental latter part of the 19th century. Yet the Moorish Arch, if not in its architecture though certainly in its symbolism, was the prototype of the much lamented Doric Arch at Euston. It set the pattern of having a grand architectural feature as a focal point for the great new enterprise of railways. On the opening day in 1830 it provided a grandstand for the people of Liverpool to witness the marshalling up of the special trains. The stairways leading down the retaining walls on both sides were equally thronged with sightseers. Although it disappeared unsung, almost without notice, it is strange that more tangible remains of it have survived than of its great successor at Euston. The cutting no longer contains any railway tracks, but the stairways on those massive retaining walls are still there, as are also the buttresses from which the arch itself was supported. In the memorable sesquicentennial year of the Liverpool and Manchester Railway it became a place of pilgrimage.

In view of all the ceremony that took place in its shadow, on Wednesday, September 15 1830, and the fame it acquired from the artists of the day, one can well ask the following question. If it had not been for the Moorish Arch at Edge Hill, would the directors of the London and Birmingham Railway ever have commissioned an architect of such eminence as P.C. Hardwick to design such a colossal entrance feature as the Doric Arch at Euston? In our present age, when conservation continues to be a very live topic, it was no more than natural that a great deal of heat should have been generated over what has been described as the 'murder' of the Euston arch; yet no one seems to have raised a murmur in later Victorian times at the demolition of the Moorish Arch. Of course, with the

Above *Liverpool: the Moorish Arch at the time of the opening of the Liverpool and Manchester Railway.* **Below** *Site of the Moorish Arch: remains of the buttresses, and the stairway leading down to the tracks* (Bob Bird Photographers).

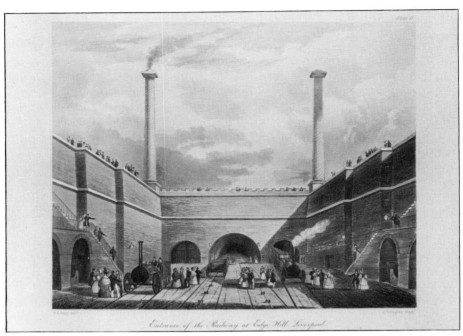

Above *The engine terminus in Wapping Cutting, 1833* (The British Tourist Authority).
Below *The same view before restoration began in time for the L & M 150th anniversary in 1979* (Bob Bird Photographers).

Above *Olive Mount cutting, just east of Edge Hill, Liverpool and Manchester Railway, as originally cut.* **Below** *Olive Mount cutting today, as widened to take additional tracks* (Bob Bird Photographers).

construction of the new passenger line from Edge Hill down into Lime Street it passed out of sight of the ordinary traveller—what happened in a deep cutting on a goods line could take place without anyone being aware of it. Its flanking towers blocked the way to having four tracks from outside to the inner excavation; but now, ironically, when its supreme historic interest is at last appreciated, the tracks have been removed and the site is derelict. Nevertheless, looking down from the top of the surviving staircase today one can well imagine how early travellers were enthralled, on seeing below the pioneer locomotives and coaching stock, and all the attendant and then-unfamiliar activity of a railway terminal station. For the first three months of the Liverpool and Manchester Railway this was the place of departure, and to reach the trains one had to descend by one or other of the stairways. Crown Street station, beyond the tunnel, was used from January 1831.

The Liverpool and Manchester Railway had certainly started something with that Moorish Arch, and the London and Birmingham had to go one better, at Euston. It needs, alas, no archaeological research to determine details of the gigantic Doric propylaeum that was built by Philip Hardwick at the entrance to the station. Its design was well documented, and became only too familiar at the time when its death-sentence was passed in the 1960s. It is not always realised, however, that twice previously there had been schemes for the complete rebuilding of Euston, in both of which the Doric propylaeum would have had to go. I have used the technical word, instead of the more familiar 'arch', because Hardwick's creation at Euston was to quote the dictionary definition: 'gateway of architectural importance'. As originally built, and clear of all other obstructions, it presented a breathtaking spectacle when seen from what was at first known as the New Road, with a wide open parade ground completely clear of any building extending from the road to the propylaeum.

This is how it struck a contemporary writer, John Britton, in 1839:

'Separating the station from the public street is the Propylaeum, or architectural gateway (improperly called a portico), with four lodges, or offices connected with it; intermediate to which, and in combination with the whole, are large, lofty and ornamental iron gates, cast by J.J. Bramah. The Propylaeum is remarkable for magnitude and simplicity of arrangement and for its strictly classical character. It is, indeed, a most successful adaptation of pure Grecian Doric; admirably suited, by the massiveness and boldness of the design and execution, for an approach to a line of communication connecting the British Metropolis with the most important towns of the Kingdom. Objections have been made, and with some appearance of reason, to the great expense of this ornamental entrance; in reply to which, it may be said that the Railway is a great national undertaking, and that the national character is, in some respects, involved in the execution of the whole. All spectators are impressed by magnitude of mass, or by highly enriched detail in public buildings; and it is often remarked by critics that the English are too parsimonious and calculating to produce either the one or the other. The following comments by a judicious writer are in unison with our own convictions:

"As a specimen of Greek architecture, this structure has not only the merit of being on a grander scale than anything of the kind yet attempted in this country, but also free from any adulteration of the style by the admixture of features, which however well they may be designed in themselves, almost invariably detract more or less from classicality of design. Here there was, fortunately, no occasion for having sash windows peeping out between Doric columns. Neither have we a severe Doric portico; correct, perhaps, and unexceptionable in itself, yet tacked on to a building of different and modern physiognomy, and to which it is merely an adjunct, and an expletive. On the contrary, the Grecian outline is preserved entire; on which account the structure exhibits itself to most advantage when viewed obliquely, so as to show its line of roof and depth, especially as the cornice is of unusually bold and new design, being not only ornamented with projecting lion heads, but crowned by a series of deep antifixae; while when beheld from a greater distance, the large stone slabs are also seen that cover the roof".'

Need one say more! I suppose it was too much to hope that as the price of land soared the open parade ground could have been kept clear, and the magnificent prospect preserved for all time. But, a mere 30 years after its first construction, some of the most prominent writers of the day had no time for it. In his celebrated work of 1868, *Rambles on Railways*, Sir Cusack Roney wrote: 'One of the oldest railways guide books published, gives exact directions how to arrive at Euston Station from other parts of the town, and we are to take special notice of "The Grand Facade at Euston Grove". The centre of it is the Doric portico built by Hardwich (sic!), used by nobody, which, however, cost share-holders no less than £40,000. No wonder, seeing that it contains not less than 75,000 cubic feet of Yorkshire freestone, several of the blocks of which, weighed upwards of thirteen tons each.'

Passing by, but not through this massive portal, we arrive at the actual station, and thence at the platforms. It was the London and North Western Railway itself that began the obscuring process by the building of the Euston Hotel. At first there were separate wings to left and right of the approach road leaving the great entrance still visible from Euston Road; but new buildings were springing up all around and, although the new gatehouses, built right out and alongside the main road, gave some dignity to the approach to the station, the once stupendous vista was gone, as was very evident from an engraving published in the *Illustrated London News* as early as 1869.

Then it only needed the intense materialism of later Victorian times to connect the two wings of the Euston Hotel, with an insignificant arch across the roadway to blank off the entire prospect. The glorious propylaeum was completely encompassed by tall buildings of the most undistinguished kind. In the flow of road traffic into and out of the central courtyard it became an incumbrance rather than the tremendous symbolic edifice it had originally been. It became even worse when the major enlargement of the station on the west side was undertaken, in 1892, and the four very long departure platforms, 12, 13, 14 and 15 were brought into service. For some reason the booking office for trains leaving from them was separated from the original one, and there was often wild confusion in the courtyard and beneath the propylaeum, when passengers arriving in cabs, or their own carriages, and going to the booking office with which they were familiar found to their annoyance that they were refused a ticket because the train went from one of the new platforms. With the usual mountains of luggage with which so many people travelled at that time, and that luggage already unloaded and having to be moved somehow over to the west platform, there were frequently moments of highly coloured language. Passengers used to the old calm and precision of Euston regarded this as an impertinence, and the seal was set upon it, when a Director turned bitterly to an operating man and said: 'You have turned Euston into a Waterloo'! As may have been gathered from the previous chapter the London and South Western terminus was not famed for the smoothness of its passenger handling facilities.

In 1895, with traffic on the line as a whole booming again, after the lengthy coal strike of 1893, and the prestige of the line enhanced by the notable acceleration of the Anglo-Scottish traffic, resulting from the exciting Race to the North, there was a great scheme for the complete rebuilding of Euston. This absorbed all the intervening property, and bought the station frontage right up to the Euston Road, as the Midland had so skilfully done at St Pancras. This, of course, would have involved the complete removal of the Doric propylaeum, and with it the Great Hall, which has so far received no more than a passing mention. Seeing how splendidly the operating men of the LNWR modernised their track layouts on other parts of the line there is no doubt that the making available of so much extra length between the foot of Camden bank and the buffer stops would have been supremely beneficial in working the traffic; but the great scheme was shelved, and the Arch remained, getting blacker and blacker with the grime of London as the years went by.

Philip Hardwick, the architect of the propylaeum was himself the son of a famous architect, and had worked under Sir William Chambers in the construction of Somerset House. Philip was born in 1792, and was thus in his mid-40s at the time of the Euston creation. It so happened that the propylaeum was the last work he did unassisted by his own son, Philip Charles. It was father and son together who designed the second architectural masterpiece of Old Euston, the Great Hall. It would have disappeared in the 1895 scheme of modernisation but, as things eventuated, it, together with the Arch, survived for another 65 years. The Great Hall was completed in 1849, after the London and Birmingham Railway had become part of the London and North Western. A contemporary account gives the following detailed and laudatory description:

'On the northern side of the outer vestibule are five entrances leading into the Central Hall. The length of this magnificent hall below the entablature is 125 feet 6 inches, the width 61 feet 4 inches, and the height from the floor to the ceiling 62 feet. At the northern end is a grand double stone curved staircase leading to the central flight, by which a beautiful vestibule 16 feet in width is reached. The entire length of the hall, from the wall of the gallery to the southern wall, is 139 feet. From the vestibule access is obtained to the general meeting room, the board room, the conference room and the gallery which runs round the hall, giving facility of communication to an infinity of offices.

'The style of architecture is Roman Ionic. The ceiling is formed of panels, deeply coffered, the bands forming the panels being enriched with a double guilloche pattern, and is supported at the northern end by four double columns, and at the southern end by four single corresponding columns each 24 feet 7 inches in height, without the base. The columns are highly finished and have the appearance of beautifully polished red granite, with white marble capitals and bases. The hall is lighted by attic windows above the entablature between which are massive consoles to support the ceiling. The consoles are elaborately designed and are supported upon lions heads. The mouth of each lion holds a ring, by which are suspended bunches of fruit and flowers.

'The area of the hall and the staircase is built of the best Craigleith stone, and the walls, of grey Martin's cement, are painted to simulate granite. Eight bas-reliefs adorn the panels in the corners of the hall. They typify London,

Above left *Euston: the Doric Arch.* **Above right** *Euston: the magnificent roof of the now demolished Great Hall* (British Railways).

Liverpool, Manchester, Birmingham, Carlisle, Chester, Lancaster and Northampton, the chief cities and boroughs with which the London and North Western Railway communicates. The large group in alto-rilievo over the door leading into the general meeting room is a picturesque and effective composition. It consists of the figure of Britannia, seated, with her left arm resting on the head of a stupendous lion, whilst at her left is the prow of a ship; on the right she is supported by a life-size figure representing the Arts and Sciences, and on the left by a figure of Mercury of equal stature.'

P.C. Hardwick was an artist in watercolours as well as an architect, and he has left an exquisite painting of the hall as it was in the early 1850s, which I was privileged to have reproduced as frontispiece to one of my earlier books*. But I recall the place no less as a quiet and leisurely waiting room, with access on one side to the very dignified little tea room, and on the other to the station dining room—so far removed, both of them were, from the rush and brashness of the modern self-service buffets, characteristic of railway stations today. I am thinking now of the 1930s, and at that time Old Euston was once again under sentence of death. This time it was the LMS that had grandiose plans for the complete rebuilding of the station, and needless to say the demolition of both the Doric Arch and the Great Hall; but this time it was the onset of the Second World War that stayed the act of execution. Hamilton Ellis in his book *Four Main Lines* has picturesquely described the situation:

'On July 12, 1938 the late Lord Stamp, sitting in the shareholders' room, turned a switch which closed a circuit and blasted out some 100,000 tons of limestone far away in Caldon Low Quarries, providing raw material for the new

The Railways of Britain—Past and Present.

station. Sir Francis Joseph, one of the LMS directors, selected a choice block, which was to be made into the foundation stone. The war came, the bombs came; Lord Stamp, who had said he would never forsake his Victorian house in Beckenham until he was blown out of it, was fatefully taken at his word. But Old Euston stood fast as Craigellachie!'

When the time did eventually come for the destruction of these two priceless monuments the act aroused a tremendous amount of acrimony, sentiment and bitterness. It is no part of the archaeological approach to the subject to suggest how the station might have been reconstructed so as to include both the Doric Arch and the Great Hall. As one much involved in modern railway operation, and equally a lover of history, I have derived a great deal of amusement in trying to work out an acceptable scheme. I am sure that given the necessary goodwill it could have been done. But having said that, however, and having had occasion to spend much time in the rushing modern purlieus of the New Euston, I wonder if, in the present context, the Doric Arch and the Great Hall would not stand as rather pathetic anachronisms, quite out of keeping with an age from which the one-time leisure, dignity and opulence of main line railway travelling has entirely disappeared.

Euston, starkly utilitarian as it is today, still remains one of the principal gateways to the north, and at the furthest place to which its through carriages and sleeping cars progress, Inverness, there was another remarkable layout of great interest to the railway archaeologist. Unlike Euston, unlike even the Moorish Arch at Liverpool, the centre of attraction in the Highland capital has never been frequented by the travelling public at all. The Highland Railway began very modestly. The original master plan of building a line from Inverness over the very crest of the Grampian Mountains and down to Perth was deferred, as a result of ridicule; but the stout-hearted projectors were not to be denied, and in their second attempt they proceeded by guile, promoting a line from Inverness no farther than Nairn, 15 miles, followed by the so-called Inverness and Aberdeen Junction Railway, authorised in July 1856, and to take over the working of the Inverness and Nairn. Together these made up a main line 55 miles long, from Inverness to Keith and when, in July 1861, the Inverness and Perth Junction Railway was also authorised, with a line from Forres southward over the Mountains, it was evident that provision would have to be made at

Inverness: the elevation of the running shed (British Railways).

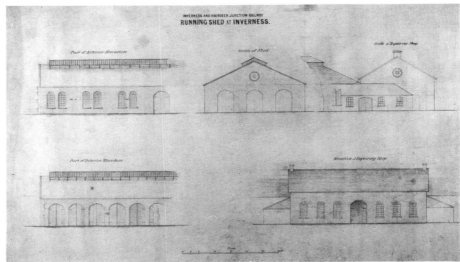

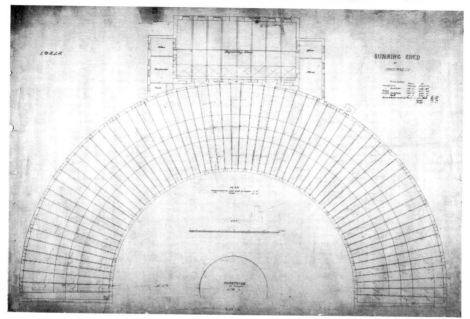

Inverness: plan for the running shed (British Railways).

Inverness for stabling and servicing many more locomotives. The Inverness and Nairn Railway had opened for business with no more than two. In October 1862 construction of a running shed to house 20 locomotives was authorised and, although the passenger station at Inverness was slowly developing into an undistinguished hotch-potch, Joseph Mitchell, the engineer, produced a very striking layout for the running shed, including some quite remarkable architecture.

The shed was of the round-house type, with all the stabling tracks spreading out like the spokes of a wheel from a central turntable. Each bay in the shed was entered through an arch in the building, and the locomotive thus ensconced could be concealed from public gaze by closing a pair of folding doors. The original provision for 20 engine roads was actually increased to 24 before the building was finished, and this formed only two-thirds of a complete circle. The opening was at the eastern end, and in the middle of it was a very splendid water-tower. I have seen it suggested this was originally intended to be the portal to a round-house extended to full circle; but, seeing the beauty of the architectural design of that water-tower, much of which would have been concealed if the shed buildings had been extended to link up with it, I can hardly think this was the case. The original shed was extended to provide 31 bays, and this left room on each side of the water-tower for one track.

I saw the shed at various stages in its life. Just after the grouping, in 1923, the folding doors on each shed road had been removed. While these were no doubt a protection against the severity of Highland winter weather their usefulness virtually ceased with the introduction of 4-6-0 locomotives, especially Peter Drummond's 'Castle' class of 1900, with their double-bogie tenders. These measured 61 feet over buffers and, with one of them inside, their extremity stood out towards the turntable too far to enable the doors to be closed. The shed itself was a fine piece of masonry with some artistically styled windows to each engine bay on the outer wall. After the doors had gone, the arches on the inner wall remained until some time after the Second World War. The standard main line engines for the Highland Line were then the ex-LMS Stanier Black Five 4-6-0. It was usual to park these in the shed with their front-ends inside, and the rear end of their tenders projecting outwards. The roads were, of course, converging towards the turntable, and space between those projecting tenders became confined. So the stonework of the arches was removed, and the roof on the inside arc of the shed supported on steel columns. This change, practical politics though it may have been, took away much of the former character of that inner enclave. The central turntable had originally been boarded completely over, providing a convenient walk-area for the men; and many Highland engines were posed for their photographs on that turntable. In later years, however, when the timbers of that flooring needed renewal, the whole covering was removed and the turntable worked in an open pit of conventional appearance.

The water-tower was quite an architectural masterpiece in the classical style. Joseph Mitchell, a townsman of Inverness put some beautiful work into the bridges of the Highland main line, as are still to be seen in heavy service today in the Pass of Killiecrankie and at Struan where the railway strides across both the River Garry and the highway, in a single leap, as it were. In each case the stonework was enriched by little touches of ornamental castellation. Although no passengers and only privileged visitors were likely to see it, his running-shed water-tower was another little gem. How water was got up into the large static tank that spanned the track beneath, and extended to the limit of the building on either side, I do not know; but locomotives placed their tenders beneath the arch, and there was always a plentiful supply. The round-house and its water-tower were still in use when the diesels began to replace steam, but in the new age, running *sheds* were no longer needed. Servicing facilities for the diesels were more akin to roadside filling stations on the highway. In the overriding need to secure maximum utilisation of the motive-power stud there was no time for locomotives to go 'on shed', and be tucked cosily for the night behind closed doors. Across the tracks, on the site of the old Lochgorm locomotive works, a servicing and fuelling plant for the diesels was erected and the old running shed abandoned. No Scottish counterpart of Sir John Betjeman arose to campaign for preservation, and so the round-house and the classic water-tower with it

Inverness: the ornamental water-tower (Locomotive Publishing Co).

were demolished and the site cleared to make a municipal car park!

One can think of many ways of demolishing old railway edifices, but the Luftwaffe made short work of the Central Station at Barrow-in-Furness one night in the early spring of 1941. Arising from the piecemeal way in which the Furness Railway had come into existence, Barrow itself was a terminus until the year 1882. The original line ran from Kirkby-in-Furness to Piel Pier, and from this there was a branch that terminated alongside the Walney Channel, and served the dock sides, and various industrial concerns. When the several small individual railway enterprises were connected up to make a through line from Carnforth to Whitehaven and beyond, Barrow was still at the end of a short branch served by connections from the through trains, or by trains that terminated there. In 1882, however, a short link $7\frac{1}{2}$ miles long was completed which permitted continuous running from north to south through Barrow and, at an addition of £15,000, a new Central station was built. This had four tracks, but only two of these passed under the all-over roof. The remaining two platforms were out in the open. Furthermore the imposing roof that covered the two main platforms was rather short, and trains that were of any length extended into the open, front and rear, without any shelter. By the time the Nazi bombers had finished with it, however, the fashion for large all-over roofs had passed and reconstruction, when the time came, provided conventional awnings.

No mention of all-over roofs would be complete without a reference to the standard style adopted by Isambard Kingdom Brunel for many of the smaller stations on the various extensions of the Great Western, into South Wales and the West of England. His philosophy, even in the case of stations as large as Reading or Newton Abbot, was to concentrate all station business in a single block of buildings, having ready access to the town. All trains stopping at the station would use a platform adjacent to this building block whether they were travelling east or west. Crossover roads would be laid in to facilitate direct movement from either direction. That such stations became very difficult to operate, as traffic increased, is apart from the present point, which is that Brunel constructed all-over roofs from the main business block to cover many, if not all the through lines running parallel. In cross section those roofs were designed with a very shallow angle as though to fit the pediment shape at the

Bristol Temple Meads: the original Brunel station, now in process of restoration.

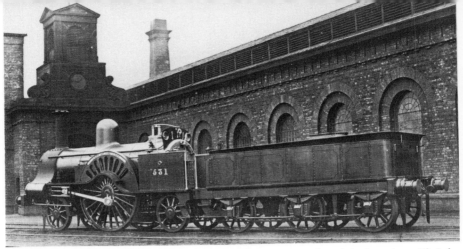

Crewe works: the ornamental clock tower at the entrance to the original works, with John Ramsbottom's famous Lady of the Lake *locomotive in front* (British Railways).

outer ends. Windsor was a striking example in this style for a terminal station while Exeter St Thomas remained for a very long time as a roof spanning from two working platforms, across two busy running lines.

At Bristol Temple Meads, and somewhat similarly at Bath, Brunel built major roofs that could be described as of the hammer-beam type. The one at Bath has long since been removed, but Temple Meads remains, though covering no more than a car park. It is a curious piece of work, because although it has every appearance of a hammer-beam it is not so; the hammer-beam members are no more than decorative timber work, by which Brunel apparently felt it was necessary to disguise the basic structural fabric of the roof. In J.C. Bourne's famous and magnificently illustrated work, *The History and Description of the Great Western Railway*, the construction is described thus:

'The roof is composed of a series of 44 ribs, 22 on a side, and placed 10 feet apart, each of which is constructed somewhat like the jib of a crane, that is to say, of a long arm, projecting far and rising high into the air, and a short arm or tail, which in heavy cranes is either tied down or loaded. In the present case, the iron columns which divide the central space from the aisles are the fulcra or crane posts upon which the arms rest. The long arm or jib extends to the centre and ridge of the roof, and there meets its fellow from the opposite side, while the short arm or tail is carried backward to form the roof of the aisle, to the outer wall of which it is held down by a strong vertical tie passing some way down. The whole is then planked over diagonally, and is intended to be filled up, and decorated to suit the rest of the building'.

The decoration that looked like hammer beams took none of the basic loads on the structure. At Bath Brunel used the same principle of major construction but the decorative camouflage was different. What Bourne called the *fulcra*, or crane posts, were similarly spaced and apparently quite near to the outer edges of the platforms. These, of course, were vital parts of the structure and, spaced only 10 feet apart, must have been something of an inconvenience to passengers when boarding trains. Nowadays the tracks passing through Bath are on sufficient of a curve to require a speed restriction to 30 mph for non-stopping trains; but that the original roofed in part of the station was straight can be seen from the buildings on each side of the line, which structurally remain as Brunel built them.

Chapter 7

Dismantled and replaced viaducts

In seeking out details of the railway viaducts that have gone, either because the lines themselves have been closed, or because the wear and tear of traffic and climatic conditions have required their replacement by more modern structures, one becomes utterly fascinated by the skill with which timber was used as a principal material. Of all British engineers I.K. Brunel will no doubt be best remembered in this connection, but in the design of heavy load carrying structures he was certainly not the first in England. Nor were the timber trestles that gave so picturesque a touch to the broad-gauge lines in South Devon and Cornwall his own first, for carrying trains. It is true that in carrying a country lane across Sonning Cutting he had evolved an exact prototype of some of his later railway viaducts in the West Country, but his own first essay, and one of a totally different kind, came in 1840 at Bath, where he used a design that had been pioneered on the continent of Europe some 30 years previously. This was the laminated timber arch, in which the laminations were bent into position.

The first use in England for a technique originally devised for road bridges was on the Newcastle and North Shields Railway, opened in 1839. In this relatively short line, of no more than about eight miles, there were deep valleys to be crossed at Ouseburn and Willington Dene, and the architect, John Green, adopted the laminated arch form of construction for two magnificent viaducts, one of five and the other of seven arches. In both viaducts the span of the arches was approximately 115 feet, though there were some slight variations, as between individual arches on the two viaducts. On both, the arches consisted of three parallel ribs. They each consisted of 14 layers of planks 3 inches thick and 11 inches broad, so assembled and braced together to form a rib $3\frac{1}{2}$ feet thick and 22 inches wide. The planks, which were each pre-treated with an anti-rot injection process, then known as Kyanising, were between 20 and 45 feet long, and were bent to form the designed curve of the arch. They were supported on massive stone piers, and the spandrel space was filled with an artistic assembly of radiating and vertical struts. Both viaducts were exceedingly handsome. Ouseburn, quite near to Newcastle, came to form part of the East Coast main line from London to Edinburgh, when the Newcastle and Berwick Railway was authorised in 1845, and its amalgamation with the North Shields line was subsequently arranged. The Ouseburn viaduct carried the main line traffic until 1869, when the laminated timber arches were replaced by iron ones.

These two viaducts attracted much attention in the engineering profession because, even before they were brought into service, the architect's son,

Benjamin, read a paper on their design at the 1838 meeting of the British Association for the Advancement of Science. Brunel was also a member of the Association and when, in 1840, construction of the skew bridge over the Avon at Bath was held up through difficulties in obtaining the necessary iron, he produced, at short notice, an entirely different design using timber arches, for which the inspiration seemed clearly to come from John Green's work on the Newcastle and North Shields Railway. To what extent Brunel had become aware of the experience of the Bavarian highway engineers who had pioneered the laminated arch form of construction we do not know. Certainly the viaducts on the North Shields line would not have been in service long enough for one weakness to be revealed, namely that the laminations tended to separate under load, and allow water to seep in between them. Be that as it may, in designing the arches for the skew bridge at Bath he used laminations six inches thick, instead of the three-inch planks used by Green. Although, as might be imagined, there was some difficulty in bending timbers of such thickness to the designed curve of the arch the greater thickness paid off handsomely; because the general life, elsewhere, was 25 years for these laminated timber arched viaducts and the skew bridge at Bath lasted for 38 years, under what was probably the heaviest traffic to which a bridge of this kind was ever submitted.

The details of the skew bridge at Bath show Brunel's innate sense of the practical in designing for heavy duty, and equally his superb artistry in presentation. The bridge had two 89-foot spans, each with six parallel ribs at five foot centres. The ribs themselves each had five laminations, six inches thick, fastened together with bolts and iron straps. The planks, if one could call members so thick as six inches by that name, were of the very finest Memel pine, and were, of course, thoroughly Kyanised before incorporation in the structure. (It may be explained that the term 'Kyanising' was derived from the inventor of the process, John N. Kyan, in every way the pioneer of the modern processess of timber preservation.) Brunel's artistry was shown in the decorative cast iron spandrel frames that he inserted on the four outside arches, these frames also supporting the timber parapets. The inner spandrels contained cross-ties and struts that contributed to the massive nature of the bridge as a whole. Despite this, and its essential serviceability, the bridge had an elegance appropriate to the architecture of Bath itself.

Brunel's first application of timber frameworks to the viaducts, necessary for crossing the deep valleys athwart the course of the South Devon Railway, was not very successful; but the design he adopted may have been influenced by his intention, originally, to use the atmospheric system of propulsion rather than steam locomotives. The massive masonry piers were built up to rail deck level, and the timber frameworks between the piers were part truss and part horizontal beams. The one at Ivybridge was perhaps outstanding. Not only did it have a maximum height of 114 feet above the river Erme below, but it was on a considerable curve. The atmospheric system did not extend farther west than Totnes, and it had been discarded as a failure long before the line was opened for traffic over the very hilly section west of that town. With the passage of steam locomotives over viaducts, such as that at Ivybridge, considerable lateral stresses would have been imparted and it is not without significance that all five viaducts of this type on the South Devon Railway, opened in 1849, had been replaced within 14 years.

Next in this catalogue of viaducts that have been replaced is, strangely

Robert Stephenson's great Britannia Bridge over the Menai Strait: the opening ceremony in March 1850 (British Railways).

enough, Robert Stephenson's great Britannia Tubular Bridge over the Menai Strait, damaged irreparably by the results of a foolhardy, yet quite trifling, accident. It is incredible to think that a structure of such colossal proportions could have been distorted to such an extent as to make total replacement the only course after a small fire, irresponsibly started near one end by some children, allegedly searching for bird nests. The conception, design and erection of the Britannia Tubular Bridge has been documented perhaps more fully than any other work of the Victorian railway age. For those who would study it in the most minute detail there is the classic contemporary work of Edwin Clark, assistant to Robert Stephenson for the ironwork and for the operations for floating and raising the tubes. Remarkably, this book was published to coincide with the completion of the job, and the opening of the Chester and Holyhead Railway, and it included a folio volume of plates and drawings illustrative of the progress of the work.

In Parry's *Railway Companion from Chester to Holyhead*, published in 1848, a civil engineer of the day, George Grove by name, contributed an eye-witness account of the progress of the work, from which the following passages may be quoted:

'We recommend those of our readers who have nerve and resolution enough, to climb one of the land-towers, and, advancing as nearly as possible to the end of the stonework, in the opening intended for the tube, to look across the gulf between their standing place and the Britannia tower, and then form their own judgement. It is the only way of really appreciating the vastness and daring of the undertaking, and is well worth a trial. From this height the appearance of the four large tubes on their platforms is very striking.

'. . . We shall help our London readers to some more intimate knowledge of the huge size of these great structures, if we remind them that "The

Monument'' would not reach half the distance they are now looking over, and if one of the tubes could be set up on its end, it would be high enough to overtop not only the cross of Saint Paul's, but the far-famed Salisbury spire itself.'

The forthcoming operation of floating the great 470-foot long tubes from their moorings out into mid-stream, and into place between the towers, was eagerly anticipated and explanatory details of the procedure were prepared beforehand for the benefit of the many sightseers expected, and for representatives of the press. When the appointed day dawned the weather was very stormy, with strong winds and, because of the broad target that one of the tubes would provide for the wind, and because of the risk of getting it out of control once out in the middle of the waterway, Stephenson decided to postpone the operation. Next morning the arrival of the daily newspapers caused great merriment among his staff, for some of those papers contained highly coloured accounts of how the first of the tubes had been successfully floated into place!

Until the evening of May 23 1970 one would have thought that the great bridge was there in perpetuity. It had carried increasing heavy locomotives and trains for more than a hundred years and, with careful maintenance, seemed good for at least another hundred, until a small fire, just inside the abutment at the Caernarvonshire end, fanned by a strong wind, caught the wooden thickly tarred roof of the tubes and in a very short time the interiors were a roaring inferno. The linings were completely destroyed, and the intense heat so distorted Stephenson's historic wrought iron tubes as to make them useless henceforth. The reconstruction, using the original towers, is one of the most beautiful bridges of recent times; and while we can deeply regret the disappearance of the 'tubes', they did at least go down 'in action' as it were, rather than suffer the ignominy of the deliberate demolition that befell the Moorish Arch and the classic water tower of Inverness.

The timber viaducts of Brunel on the Cornwall Railway, between Plymouth and Falmouth, provide a study of rare fascination. Fortunately their technical details have been very carefully documented. In the 1930s the Great Western Railway had a divisional engineer at Plymouth, in the person of H.S.B. Whitley, who was a dedicated enthusiast for them, as well as being a man of the

Cornwall Railway: timber trestle viaduct by Brunel, at Forder, over one of the tidal creeks of the Lynher River, near Saltash (British Railways).

Cornwall Railway: timber trestle viaduct near St Germans, 1899 (British Railways).

highest professional skill and attainments. I had the pleasure of meeting him when he had moved one step higher on the ladder of promotion, and was divisional engineer at Wolverhampton. When the last of the timber viaducts in the West Country was scheduled for replacement, in 1932, he wrote a scholarly article, copiously illustrated, in *The Railway Engineer*, describing the details of construction of the various types used by Brunel, how they were maintained, and—no less importantly to the engineer's department of the railway—how they were dismantled when the time came for them to be dismantled. In many locations new stone viaducts carrying a double line of railway were built alongside and, after the timbers of the old viaducts had been removed, the original piers were left in situ. It is remarkable that in the 65 miles of the Cornwall Railway, from Plymouth to Falmouth, there were no fewer than 42 of these timber trestle viaducts and, all except one, carried only a single line of railway.

Brunel had no overall standard design and some of the most interesting were those crossing the tidal creeks between Saltash and St Germans, which had timber legs. On the West Cornwall Railway, which extended from Penwithers Junction, near Truro, to Penzance, the original viaducts were of extraordinary fragile appearance, with what appeared to be the flimsiest of timber legs and, at a fairly early date in the history of the line, masonry piers were built to replace the lower legs. The 34 viaducts between Plymouth and Truro were all built in 1859 and those on the continuation of the Cornwall Railway to Falmouth, in 1863. The West Cornwall Railway, originally a completely isolated narrow-gauge line was constructed entirely in 1852 and had nine timber viaducts in its length of 26 miles. On the main line the last of the timber viaducts were, with one exception, on the tidal creek section between Saltash and St Germans, and five there, including the dainty looking Nottar and St Germans itself, survived till 1908, by which time the inland deviation line was complete. When I travelled to Falmouth in 1924, however, all eight viaducts on the branch were still in service, including the lofty Ponsanooth, 139 feet high, and the longest and last to survive, Collegewood, just outside Falmouth. This was 954 feet long and 100 feet high. It was not replaced until 1934.

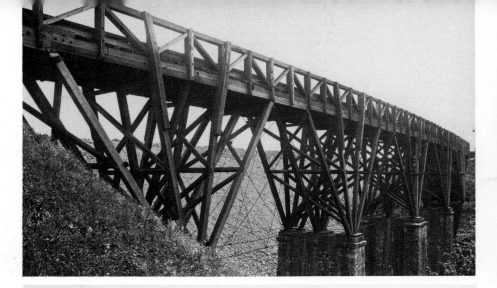

From Brunel we pass on to the work of another noted civil engineer of the day, Thomas Bouch. I have referred earlier in this book to the projecting of the South Durham and Lancashire Union Railway, between Barnard Castle and Tebay on the London and North Western main line. Some mountainous country had to be negotiated and, in crossing deep valleys, Bouch used an elegant, indeed daring, form of construction with the spans in wrought iron lattice girders and the piers in cast iron. That these latter attained a maximum height of 196 feet at Belah, on the western side of the summit, my use of the word 'daring' can be understood. Each pier was composed of six cast iron columns, 12 inches in diameter, arranged in two parallel lines of three each, and braced together with cross girders at intervals of 15 feet vertically and also by horizontal and diagonal wrought iron tie bars. The width at the base was 50 feet but the columns tapered gradually inwards until the piers were only 22 feet wide at the top, to carry a double-line railway. With a total length of 1,040 feet and 60-foot spans, a total of 15 piers were needed.

An outstanding feature of the viaduct was the speed with which it was built—in no more than four months from laying the foundation stone, in November

Left *Detail of a Brunellian trestle viaduct, with the timber struts resting on masonry piers near Penryn on the Falmouth branch* (British Railways). **Below left** *Pascoe viaduct, in 1923, when arrangements were in progress for its replacement by an embankment, as seen on left. The branch train for Falmouth is crossing* (British Railways).

Right *A track level view of Brunel's tubular girder bridge over the River Wye, at Chepstow: a prototype for the famous Albert Bridge at Saltash. This bridge at Chepstow has now been rebuilt* (British Railways).

1857, to completion. Gilkes Wilson of Middlesbrough was the contractor, and a couplet written at the time ran thus: 'To future ages these lines will tell who built this structure o'er the dell. Gilkes Wilson, with his eighty men, raised Belah's Viaduct o'er the glen.' I shall not forget an occasion when I had an engine pass and rode on the footplate of an old North Eastern 0-6-0 over this lone, fascinating line, and the eerie feeling when we got on to that immensely tall but very slender viaduct. But the line has been closed for some time now, and the viaduct dismantled.

Belah had a more peaceful end, albeit at the hands of a demolition gang, than that most notorious of all Bouch's creations, the first Tay Bridge. Brunel always said he disliked cast iron, and avoided using it wherever he could. Bouch seemed to love it, to the extent of using it when it was not really suitable. In the design and construction of the great viaducts on the line from Barnard Castle to Tebay he was well served by his distinguished assistant, Robert H. Bow, and by Gilkes Wilson, his main contractor, and the structures withstood the wildest of north country weather for upwards of a hundred years. They would no doubt have lasted a good deal longer if the line had remained open. Bouch was not so

fortunate in the first Tay Bridge. Again, as at Belah and Deepdale, he used cast iron columns for the main uprights, but the girder work was insufficiently braced against the effect of heavy cross-winds. Not only this, but the way that bracing was secured, was fundamentally dangerous. The diagonal members were attached to the vertical columns at small lugs, cast integrally with the columns thus putting those small projectors in tension, and to crown all, the fixing bolts were made with a clearance, rather than a tight fit. Thus, during the passage of a train, there would always be a certain amount of slogger. This was just asking for trouble.

At that period in history, mechanical engineering practice, and with it the use of iron in large structures, depended to a remarkable extent on what has been termed the 'factor of ignorance'. There was no great bank of accumulated knowledge by which detailed stress analysis could be carried out. Robert Stephenson admitted that in designing the great Britannia Tubular bridge if his calculations showed that for a particular function one bolt, one rivet, or one chain was necessary, he invariably used two. Bouch did otherwise, and in a very exposed locality like the crossing of the Firth of Tay he took little, if any, account of the prevailing ignorance of the effects of wind pressure. The first Tay Bridge was designed to carry no more than a single line of rails and, while the piers of his great viaducts on the Barnard Castle-Tebay line were tapered outwards from top to bottom, on the Tay Bridge they were parallel.

Many eminent mechanical engineering designers have experienced the hazards of shifting cores in cast iron members. Robert Stephenson suffered from it in casting the first cylinders for the *Rocket* locomotive. In the cylinders his firm made for Timothy Hackworth for the *Sans Pareil*, which was to compete in the Rainhill trials in 1829, the same happened; unhappily the defect was not discovered until it was too late, when the engine began to run and burst one of her cylinders. For the main supporting columns of the Tay Bridge Bouch employed a local foundry, the quality of whose work was afterwards shown to have been altogether questionable. Regrettably, too, Bouch seems to have made no provision for the careful invigilating of the work, presumably imagining that he had, in Dundee, a contractor of the skill, experience and integrity of Gilkes Wilson. It was far otherwise! The cores shifted during the casting of those main columns, leaving the thickness of metal perilously thin on one side and thick on the other. As for those feeble little lugs for attaching the cross-stays, some fell off during the casting process. To save the expense of casting new columns, the atrocious expedient of 'burning' them on was adopted. It was a marvel the bridge lasted as long as it did. It was opened to traffic in May 1878. Just over a year later Queen Victoria travelled over it on her way to Balmoral, and while in Scotland she knighted Thomas Bouch. On December 28 1879, at the height of a great gale, the high girders over the navigable part of the firth collapsed taking with them the 5.27 pm mail train from Burntisland to Dundee and, to their deaths, the 78 persons on board.

In the days of mechanical signalling, before the invention of route indicators,

Opposite page top *Belah viaduct, South Durham and Lancashire Union line. A photograph of a Darlington to Penrith train in 1960, not long before the line was closed and the viaduct dismantled.* **Centre** *Deepdale viaduct, South Durham and Lancashire Union line, near Barnard Castle* (Ian S. Pearsall). **Bottom** *The ill-fated and ill-designed first Tay Bridge* (British Railways).

the approaches to many large junction and terminal stations were marked by huge arrays of signals on gantries spanning the tracks. Some of these were of definite structural distinction, but one, on the southern approach to Rugby, by the London and North Western Railway, had a style and history of its own. It was at that point that the loop line passing through Northampton drew alongside the main line and, to regulate traffic into the various through and platform lines ahead, and provide the slotted signals for the box at the north end of the station, a fine array of no less than 22 semaphore arms had been erected. Then, in 1899, the Great Central built their hotly contested London Extension line, and this was planned to cross the North Western main line at right angles, south of Rugby station and immediately behind the great signal gantry. The GCR viaduct was to be a massive lattice-girdered structure, forming a very prominent and confusing backdrop to the LNWR signals. This, of course, could not be tolerated, and so a condition was imposed upon the Great Central requiring them to pay for a duplication of all 22 semaphores at such a height above the existing assembly as to ensure a 'sky background', and to pay the cost of maintaining the upper 22 arms, their posts and operating gear. This great double gantry lasted until the electrification of the London Midland main line, when colour light signals replaced semaphores; and now the former Great Central viaduct has gone too, with the closing of that line.

The inception and building of the Barry Railway was one of the later romances of British railway history. How it came into existence in 1884, because of the dissatisfaction of important coal owners and shippers with the inadequacy of existing facilities in South Wales, seems extraordinary today, in view of the swarm of local railways that were then operating in the area. But that swarm was not enough, and the Act of Incorporation provided for the construction of a large coal exporting facility at what was then the rural village of Barry. In fact the original name of the undertaking was the Barry Dock and Railways Company, but this was changed simply to the Barry Railway in 1891. So, amid the existing swarm of railways in South Wales the Barry spread its tentacles to develop an enormous traffic of its own, relieving the congestion that was steadily choking the Taff Vale and the Rhymney Railways. Its connecting

Crumlin viaduct: a spectacular structure in the Welsh valleys, now demolished.

The viaduct over the Tyne at Wylam Junction, now removed.

lines were most skilfully planned but, nevertheless, involved some heavy engineering works in the mountain valleys. It had linked into the Rhymney Railway at Penrhos Junction, and by running powers reached Caerphilly, and by an Act obtained in 1898, it set out to build a northern extension to join the Brecon and Merthyr Railway in the Rhymney valley above Bedwas.

In crossing the broad valley near Llanbradach, the Barry Railway built a viaduct that was one of the largest and most spectacular of all those in the Welsh Valleys. It was 2,400 feet long, with 11 lattice girder spans resting on brick towers, rising to 125 feet above the valley floor. It was spectacular as much in the simple massive utilitarianism of the design as in its great length. It was opened for traffic in January 1905, only for coal; but this, of course, was the life blood of the Barry Railway, in this case tapped from the Brecon and Merthyr line, and taken expeditiously down to Barry Docks instead of its getting enmeshed below Bedwas in the congestion that prevailed around Newport. So for 20 years, while the Barry Railway prospered, the coal trains rolled across the great Llanbradach viaduct; but after the grouping, when the railway became a constituent of the enlarged Great Western, and the decline of the coal industry in South Wales, the new owners obtained Parliamentary powers to abandon the line.

Demolition of the great viaduct, and also that of the smaller, but similarly designed, Penyrheol viaduct took place in 1937. Llanbradach contained about 3,150 tons of steel and, at the time when the national re-armament programme was increasing in intensity, such a tonnage was invaluable. The method of removing the girders was as spectacular as the viaduct itself. The construction was of the lattice girder deck type in which each main girder was immediately below one of the tracks. The decking parapet rails, and all the top surface material was first removed. Then jacks were inserted under the inward flanges of the main girders on the top of the piers, and the girders tilted outwards until they overbalanced and crashed 90 feet to the ground. It was a breathtaking sight, because in each case the girders turned a complete somersault in falling, with the bottom flange finishing furthest from the piers.

Chapter 8

Classics in brick and stone that remain

It is a happy situation when great monuments of past endeavour continue to play a vital part in the life and commerce of the modern age, so unobtrusively, with such continuing and unfailing reliability that their existence is apt to be taken entirely for granted. Of course the building of great arched viaducts was no new art at the beginning of the railway age, and the established professional engineers of the day were inclined to regard the men striving to project the first railways as so many ill-educated amateurs, virtually beneath the notice of the élite of the profession. It was certainly in this light that Sir John Rennie and his brother, George, viewed the activities of George Stephenson and the young men who were gathering round him. But, as things turned out, the Rennies, despite their high professional status, secured very little in the way of railway building assignments. They strove mightily, by back-stage manoeuvres and rhetoric derogatory of Stephenson, to get their plans accepted for the Liverpool and

One of the earliest, and now best known of railway main line overbridges: the magnificent stone skew bridge over the Liverpool and Manchester Railway at Rainhill station—a modern photograph (Bob Bird Photographers).

Manchester Railway, all eventually to no avail; and in the end it was only the Brighton line that remains as an example of their railway projecting.

History has shown that the 'amateurs', the novices of the north, who no doubt studied contemporary constructional practice most assiduously, proved very apt pupils. Not only did George Stephenson's two most brilliant assistants, his son, Robert, and Joseph Locke, build between them a greater mileage of railway than anyone else, but they included in their great main lines vast structures that not only fulfilled their immediate purpose, but which stand solid and enduring beneath the ceaseless passage of the traffic of today. When he designed the great viaduct that carried the Grand Junction Railway across the River Weaver, 16 miles north of Crewe, could Locke have foreseen the day when, in an unprecedented density of line occupation, the 25 kV electric trains would be sweeping across it at 100 mph! Superficially one could assume that he and his contemporaries built better than they knew, or that they were applying the principle adopted by Robert Stephenson in the design of the Britannia Tubular Bridge, referred to in the previous chapter, of doubling up on the calculated proportions. At first thought this would seem to be the simplest explanation of the successful longevity of all these early structural masterpieces. There were, however, at the beginning of the Railway Age, many outstanding examples of masonry or brick-arched bridges to be seen in Great Britain, the most recent by that great master, Thomas Telford; and the proportions of these were apparent. Furthermore, in theory such structures were statically indeterminate, and the proportions had been built up largely by experience. Above all, the loads imparted to the arches by the travelling loads were relatively small compared to that of the weight of the structure itself; and even in the vast

The Chester and Holyhead Railway, engineered by Robert Stephenson, at Penmaen Mawr headland. The line 'in the sea' was originally carried on a 'sea wall' built in 1846, but this was washed away, and the viaduct substituted in 1848. This latter was afterwards replaced by a massive stone arched viaduct of 13 arches, now hardly visible from the modern highway (itself on a viaduct), built far out from the avalanche-prone mountain side.

Chester and Holyhead line, LNWR: how the line was carried through the ancient town wall at Conway.

transition of railway traffic, from the tiny little steam locomotives and four-wheeled carriages to the 100 mph trains of today, it still remains so.

The earliest of these great structures, still carrying heavy traffic on the main line network of British Railways, is the Sankey viaduct on the Liverpool-Manchester line. It lies roughly half-way between the two cities, and as I rode the locomotive of a 1,000-ton liner train from Garston Docks to Glasgow, before we turned north from the historic old line at Newton Junction to join the main line to the north, I thought instinctively of George Stephenson's great pioneer work. Sankey viaduct, is a characteristically massive structure, perhaps a little *too* massive, even for the traffic it has to carry today. In some of the later, and supremely beautiful, railway viaducts only a few of the piers were made thick and heavily buttressed. The rest were gracefully slender. But at Sankey not only were all of them thick and buttressed, but the footings of the piers were markedly splayed out laterally. This would suggest a 'belt and braces' philosophy on George Stephenson's part. There is no doubt that he experienced much conern over the building of this viaduct and, for a time, he was lodging in the neighbourhood to keep a close watch on its progress.

The building of the Grand Junction Railway, linking up the Liverpool and Manchester at its midpoint with the London and Birmingham, saw the beginning of that great partnership in railway construction between Joseph Locke, as engineer, and Thomas Brassey, as contractor. Locke became one of the most skilled of railway engineers, particularly in keeping costs as low as possible. This he achieved not by cheese-pairing, or skimping in his methods or materials—rather the reverse!—but in so locating his routes as to avoid great viaducts and long tunnels. Consequently there are relatively few spectacular structures on the great main lines that he designed and Brassey built. In the dawn of main line railways, when the Liverpool and Manchester line was built, the primitve state of the motive power was a live issue, and George Stephenson built that first inter-city railway as level as possible. His son, Robert, had much

Another picturesque breaching of an ancient wall: the original entry of the York and North Midland Railway into the City of York.

the same inhibiting factors in mind with the London and Birmingham; and with its great excavations and long tunnels it cost £46,000 a mile at current prices. Locke and Brassey built the Grand Junction for £25,000 a mile.

Perhaps their most famous joint enterprise was the Lancaster and Carlisle Railway, and it is characteristic of Locke's work that in such mountainous country it was engineered with so few major viaducts, and with no tunnels. At the very beginning the River Lune had to be crossed at Lancaster, and here the laminated timber form of arch was used in three spans each of 120 feet, with much ornamental work in the spandrels. This timber work was subsequently replaced by steel plate girders. The viaducts that remain today, superbly built in stone, are within a short distance of each other, crossing the rivers Lowther and Eamont, in the approach to Penrith from the south. Both are beautiful examples of masonry-arched construction, the first having six semi-circular arches, and the second five. With the weathering of the stone both structures blend harmoniously with the typical north-country river scenery. This, however, is no more than typical of all the splendid stonework on this famous line of railway. The smaller under-bridges are all little masterpieces of masonry, and while the only intermediate stations that remain, Oxenholme and Penrith, are quite undistinguished, the station houses at some of the smaller locations, such as Burton and Holme, Shap, Southwaite and Wreay are pleasant little dwellings in stone. They have long since ceased to function as stations and the platforms have been removed.

In building the Great Western Railway, Brunel created some of the most spectacular arched bridges that had yet been seen in Great Britain—spectacular in their use of notably flat ellliptical arches, as distinct from the semi-circular arches already referred to in this chapter, and in brick. The critics averred that these flat arches would fall down. Curiously enough, however, no one seems to have become very excited over the beautiful Wharncliffe viaduct, across the valley of the Brent near Hanwell, which had eight semi-elliptical arches, each of

Top *Hownes Gill: the viaduct that replaced the gravity worked inclines. Designed by Thomas Bouch, the architect of the ill-fated first Tay Bridge, the piers were not considered strong enough, and this photograph shows the additional buttresses being added* (Crown Copyright). **Above** *Hownes Gill viaduct in the early 1950s with a heavy freight locomotive and van crossing* (S.E. Teasdale).

70-foot span, and having a rise of only 17 feet 6 inches. The majestic proportions of this viaduct which, widened to carry four tracks instead of the original two, and now crossed by many trains daily travelling at 125 mph are, of course, not seen by passengers; but they can be seen to great advantage, across green fields, from the main road (A40) just west of the Viaduct Inn, Hanwell. It was when he applied the semi-elliptical arch design to the crossing of the Thames at Maidenhead that Brunel came most heavily under fire; for here the arches were even flatter than at Hanwell, 128-foot span with a rise of 24 feet 3 inches. The proportion of span to rise, was thus $5\frac{1}{4}$, against 4, and made the arches not only the largest, but also the flattest ever constructed in brickwork.

The story of how some settlement of the eastern arch occurred, and delighted the critics who had prophesied that the bridge would fall down, is well known. The contractor had eased back the very excellent and scientific timber centering designed by Brunel a little prematurely, before the cement was properly dry, and some settlement of the brickwork ensued. But it was easily rectified. Nevertheless some concern was felt by the directors and Brunel was persuaded to leave the centering in place. Again the critics rose in chorus, saying that the moment the centering was removed the bridge would fall down. By the middle of 1838 the contractor was anxious to take them down, but Brunel told the Board he was instructing him to leave them in place until another winter (that is of 1839-40) had passed. In the autumn of 1839, however, a violent storm *blew them down*. Brunel then revealed that for a whole year previous to this they had been eased back, and had been giving no support to the arches at all! And the arches stand firm to this day. In 1838, John Fowler, afterwards Sir John, and renowned as the joint designer of the Forth Bridge, had reported that Maidenhead Bridge was in 'a dangerous condition', and painted a very gloomy picture. But in 1890, when he was called upon to advise upon the widening of the railway to four tracks over the bridge, he added, on each side, new arches having exactly the same profile as that of Brunel. A walk along the towing path of the river underneath the bridge shows clearly the line from which the widening of the original arches was made. For those who wish to study the theoretical considerations that guided Brunel in the design of these splendid

One of Brunel's castellated tunnel entrances: Twerton, west of Bath, on the original main line of the Great Western.

arched bridges, a treatise by Professor J.B.B. Owen, in the book *The Works of Isambard Kingdom Brunel* is to be recommended.

Although Sir John Rennie and his brother were prominent in the original promoting of the railway between London and Brighton, when it actually came to doing the detail work it was John Urpeth Rastrick who was engineer; and he has left some remarkable examples of his skill in bridge design. The line south of Croydon is carried on long easy gradients, not exceeding 1 in 264, and this involved long tunnels, and a magnificent viaduct, 1,440 feet long, crossing the Ouse valley, between Balcombe and Haywards Heath. Rastrick built this in stone, with 37 semi-circular arches of 30-foot span, carried on piers that have an arched opening in their centres. There is an ornamental stone ballustrade on either side. This viaduct was completed in 1841, and carries the very heavy electric train service of today with complete satisfaction. When the line eastwards from Brighton was completed, in 1846, another very long viaduct was needed immediately on its divergence from the main line to London, within Brighton itself, and here was erected another of Rastrick's masterpieces, the London Road viaduct, which had 26 semi-circular arches, each of 30-foot span, and one larger arch over a main highway. It was entirely in brickwork, and it was said that some 8,000,000 of them were used in its construction; like the Ouse viaduct it had an ornamental parapet.

This chapter began with some reference to the lasting quality of these early railway structures and, in May 1943, the Nazi bombers, above all people, provided an astonishing demonstration of this constructional strength. In one of those annoying 'tip and run' raids to which coastal towns were subjected, a bomb from a low-flying enemy aircraft passed through a garden wall, across a road, and clean through a house, before striking and exploding against the foot of Pier 7 (from the Brighton station end) of the London Road viaduct. The pier collapsed, bringing down arches 7 and 8; but although piers 6 and 8, and the arches they support, were immediately subjected to heavy stresses that they were not designed to resist, the rest of the structure stood firm. In fact the ornamental parapets remained in position, together with the railway tracks, across the gap left by the collapse of the arches below. Appropriate temporary struts and ties were immediately applied to safeguard the piers on either side of the breach from deformation by the unprecedented shear loads imposed upon them, and the line was opened again to traffic in no more than five weeks, over temporary steel trestles. The piers and arches were completely restored in four months from the original incident.

The London and York Railway which, on obtaining its Act of Incorporation, became the Great Northern, invited Joseph Locke to be its engineer. This might have seemed an invidious position for a man who was so prominently associated with the West Coast route to Scotland—Grand Junction, Lancaster and Carlisle, not to mention the uprising Caledonian. But, in May 1844, when the invitation was extended to him, the Grand Junction was on somewhat acrimonious terms with its southern associate, the London and Birmingham, and it is believed that the Grand Junction actually urged Locke to accept the invitation of the London and York, because that line, when built, could well prove a rival and embarrassment to the London and Birmingham. Locke needed little persuasion to embark upon a great new railway enterprise and he accepted. The route he proposed in 1844, which as far north as Grantham is almost

Artistry in early railway station architecture: Stowmarket, opened in 1849, on what was then the Ipswich & Bury St Edmunds Railway, now on the main line from London to Norwich (British Railways).

exactly that of the present main line north from Kings Cross, included one major viaduct, that across the valley at Welwyn.

When the Grand Junction and the London and Birmingham were settling their differences, eventually to result in their amalgamating to form the London and North Western, Locke resigned from the 'London and York', and was succeeded by William Cubitt; but Brassey was the contractor for the London end of the line, and it was he who built the big viaduct at Welwyn, of 40 arches, 1,490 feet long, and 89 feet at it maximum height. Like the majority of the great structures of pioneer days it is carrying very fast and heavy modern traffic with complete success; but unfortunately the density of line occupation today could hardly have been forseen 130 years ago! So great and lofty a structure could not be widened to take four tracks, as Maidenhead was treated, and it could have become a serious bottle-neck but for very careful timetable planning. Traffic operation apart, however, it remains yet another monument to Brassey's work, and Cubitt's design specifications.

Another outstanding example of Cubitt's constructional work is the 100 feet high, 19-arch viaduct by which he crossed the Foord gap, high above the town of Folkestone, from which eastbound travellers get such an entrancing—or perhaps intimidating!—sight of the sea, according to what kind of sailors they are. Although it is such a prominent feature of the Folkestone scene as a work of railway engineering in the historic sense it tends to be overshadowed by the dramatic stories of the line onwards to Dover, first of all in the spectacular manner in which the way was cleared for the railway, and then from the successively exciting occasions on which the line has been blocked by prodigious falls of chalk. But as to Cubitt's pioneer work, I wonder what the conservationists of today would have said to demolishing an entire headland by explosive charges to clear the way for a railway! That is precisely what Cubitt did with the Round Down Cliff. In tunnelling through Shakespeare's Cliff, however, carrying the line in two single-track bores, he has left us, in the tall Gothic pointed profiles which provide not only a uniquely distinctive façade, but which

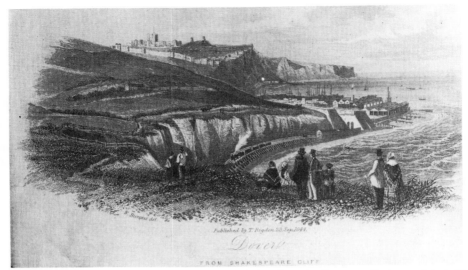

Above *A remarkable picture of Dover, in 1844, when the line was first completed. It shows twin tunnels (of the same shape as those through Shakespeare's Cliff) passing beneath the old Archcliff Fort, before reaching the terminal station on the water's edge. The fort, and the promontory on which it was built, were subsequently demolished.* **Below** *The east portal of Shakespeare's Cliff Tunnel, Dover. A photograph taken in 1960, when preparations for electrifying the line were well advanced* (Derek Cross).

continue as the profile of the bores throughout their length, the most unusual tunnel in Great Britain.

Brassey was involved in the construction of the Shrewsbury and Chester Railway, one of the two narrow-gauge lines which successfully blocked the advance of the broad gauge northward from Wolverhampton. Henry Robertson was the engineer, and he designed two magnificent viaducts, only one of which remains entirely in its original condition. The smaller of the two, over the valley of the Ceiriog, at Chirk, originally had ten stone arches, each of 45-foot span, and a spectacular laminated timber arch of 120-foot span at each end. These latter did not last very long. They were replaced by masonry arches in 1858-9. But the viaduct over the Dee, at Cefn, of 19 arches each having a span of 60 feet

Above *Folkestone: the timber viaduct originally leading to the harbour station.* **Below** *Folkestone: a picture at the same location in 1959 showing one of the last steam-hauled boat trains crossing the brick-arched viaduct that replaced the old trestle. The line is now electrified* (Derek Cross).

and a maximum height above the valley floor of 148 feet, remains today as one of the finest of Thomas Brassey's jobs. The line entered the City of Chester by running powers over the Chester and Holyhead main line, engineered by Robert Stephenson. The Shrewsbury line was ready for its opening first, and the short length of the Chester and Holyhead, from its eastern end to Saltney Junction, was actually the first part of that famous route to be brought into service, solely for the convenience of the Shrewsbury railway. This had a tragic sequel, for no more than six months later, in May 1847, when the evening train from Chester to Ruabon was crossing Stephenson's cast iron bridge over the River Dee, one of the girders fractured, in a veritable crack of doom that was heard for miles around, and the train was thrown into the river. In the circumstances the casualty list was not heavy.

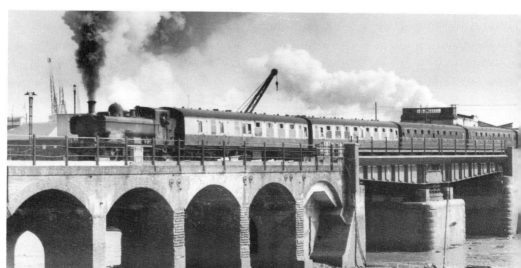

At that time Robert Stephenson was carrying an immense burden of responsibility. He was planning the great tubular bridges of the Chester and Holyhead Railway, for the Conway estuary, as well as that over the Menai Strait. In those cases, because of navigational requirements, he had to use spans of unprecedented length. Where conditions were not so demanding he used multi-arch masonry, or brick viaducts, and a beautiful and highly strategic example is that of the Royal Border Bridge, at Berwick-on-Tweed. Here the passenger station had to be located in the precincts of the old castle, on a high cliff overlooking the north bank of the river. The general profile of the line was to be continually rising from Tweedmouth, to link up with the North British Railway from Edinburgh, the first line to cross the Anglo-Scottish border. Stephenson brought the line of the Newcastle and Berwick Railway round from Tweedmouth on a great sweeping curve, on an embankment getting progressively higher, till it came to the bridge itself: 28 semi-circular arches, each of 61 foot 6 inch span, carried on elegantly proportioned piers of which the maximum height from river bed to parapet is 126 feet. The total length of the bridge is 2,160 feet and, even at 1850 prices, it cost £120,000. The curve from Tweedmouth gives passengers a fine view of the structure. At one time there was a very twisty track alignment in Berwick station that required a reduction of speed to 15 mph; but this has now been improved out of recognition, and trains from the south cross the bridge at 70 mph. As the last link in the chain of railway communication between England and Scotland on the East Coast route it was ceremonially opened by Queen Victoria on August 29 1850, and the title of 'Royal' bestowed upon it.

In Scotland, some of the finest of early masonry work was to be seen on the Highland Railway, designed by that great engineer and native of Inverness, Joseph Mitchell. In September 1867 he read a paper of the most compelling interest before The British Association, at Dundee, on *The Construction and Works of the Highland Railway* including full working drawings of 14 of the more notable bridges on the line, each one of which was a masterpiece of impeccable functional design, handsome appearance and blending wonderfully

Robert Stephenson's magnificent Royal Border Bridge, across the Tweed at Berwick, with the steam-hauled 'Flying Scotsman' of 1933 crossing. It was opened in August 1850.

with the natural surroundings. To quote Mitchell: 'In crossing so many mountain-rivers, bridges of magnitude had to be constructed, involving considerable varieties of execution. The principle of these bridges may now be described, and any peculiarity will be noticed which may have arisen during the progress of the works. It will be observed that the beds of the rivers in the north of Scotland differ in many respects from what is common in England, consisting frequently of depths of 10 or 12 feet of gravel and boulders, the solid and compacted debris of successive floods, below which if the country is of rocky formation, there is usually hard clay and then rock . . . '.

Then, referring to several places on the line where the conditions were especially difficult, he wrote: 'These points in particular required much study with repeated trial and contour levels, so as to obtain a knowledge of the precise formation of the ground, and to choose the best direction at the lowest possible cost. At the Pass of Killiecrankie the banks were so precipitous and steep that the line had to be supported by breast or retaining walls to extent of 690 lineal yards, and to the average height of 26 feet, the extreme height of one being 55 feet; and in order to carry the railway at the narrowest point in the Pass where the precipices close in, as it were, on either side, and afford scarcely any additional space beyond that occupied by the channel of the river, instead of supporting the line by breast walls, it was deemed prudent to construct a viaduct of 10 arches, 60 feet above the river, which, with a tunnel at the north end carries it successfully through the Pass'.

The resulting viaduct is one of the most beautifully situated anywhere on the railways of Great Britain, though almost completely occult from the eye of a traveller by train. One must walk, or park the car by the roadside higher up the slopes of the pass, and then scramble down to river level. Even from there the trees have grown to such an extent that the viaduct itself is almost hidden and to appreciate, at a glance, the gracious prospect that was presented when the line was opened in 1865, recourse must be made to contemporary photographs. Railway enthusiasts of an earlier generation have produced some striking pictures of trains in the LMS era crossing the viaduct, with no more than the

Joseph Mitchell's beautiful stone viaduct in the pass of Killiecrankie, on the Highland Railway. A very old photograph taken when the line was first opened in 1863.

Killiecrankie viaduct in 1938, looking very beautiful among the trees that have grown up since the railway was built.

tops of the arches showing above the trees, but these also show glimpses of Mitchell's semi-circular castellated buttresses, which he also used in the short, but equally handsome viaduct over the Garry near Struan station. This latter, striding diagonally clean across the old highway bridge, was somewhat obscured when that part of the line was widened to double track. The engineers of the Highland Railway did not adopt the technique of the Great Western, at Maidenhead, but instead erected a workmanlike, but not very picturesque, steel Warren girder taking the gorge in a single span and partly obscuring the view of Mitchell's viaduct which now carries only the northbound traffic.

Today it would seem entirely superfluous to write anything more about the structural engineering masterpieces of the Settle and Carlisle line of the former Midland Railway. Not so many years ago, however, some of us feared that the tag 'unknown in life, fortunate in its obituary' might have to be applied to the line itself. For although Charles Rous-Marten, R.E. Charlewood and Cecil J. Allen logged runs over it, and it was the scene of some strenuous dynamometer car testing of locomotives in 1923-5, there was not a single photograph of a train anywhere between Hellifield and the outskirts of Carlisle published in *The Railway Magazine* between September 1913 and September 1931. On the latter occasion, a single picture of the Thames-Clyde express at Ribblehead was a typically unimaginative example of the 'train-in-motion' cult. It could literally have been anywhere, giving not the slightest impression of the surrounding terrain. An official LMS photograph of a test run in October 1937 *did* show something of Ribblehead viaduct; but, in stormy wet weather with the steam beating down, it was not a great deal better than the 1931 effort. It was not until railway enthusiasts began to own cars as well as cameras that readers of the popular railway journals began to learn something of the delights that lay in those mighty dales. My friends Maurice Earley, Hubert Foster, Ian Pearsall, and above all my cherished collaborator the late Eric Treacy, Lord Bishop of Wakefield, blazed the trail; and then, for a while, its fame looked like being very short lived. There was a very real threat that its closure would be one of the prices to be paid for electrification of the West Coast main line over Shap.

This is no place to discuss the rights and wrongs of railway economics and politics, and one can only rejoice that the continuance of the Settle and Carlisle line seems, for the time being, secured, when British Railways are not only actively participating with the Steam Locomotives Operators Association in the regular running of excursion trains over it, but are advertising its attractions as 'The most spectacular main line in England', in a handsomely produced descriptive leaflet. So countless enthusiasts have come to know the mountain grandeur of those mighty dales, and the incomparably wild settings in which the great viaducts of Ribblehead, Denthead, Arten Gill, Dandry Mire, Lunds,

Below *The great viaduct at Ribblehead on the Settle and Carlisle line of the Midland Railway, with a modern diesel-hauled train crossing. It was opened in 1876. The mountain in the background is Ingleborough, immortalised by 'Jeanie Deans' in her walk to London in* The Heart of Midlothian *as that 'muckle flat-topped hill'* (British Railways). **Bottom** *Arten Gill: one of the most picturesque of the viaducts on the Settle and Carlisle line.*

Aisgill, Smardale and Ormside were built in 1875-6. Its significance is epitomised in the preamble to the BR leaflet previously referred to: 'The Settle and Carlisle Railway serves today as part of British Rail's Inter-City network and also as a magnificent monument to Victorian engineering'. The steam-hauled excursion trains usually include in their schedules stops to enable their patrons to take photographs of the locomotives, but not to wander further afield. Fortunately, however, most of the major constructional works are readily accessible from nearby roads, and in relative solitude and in the bracing mountain air the massive elegance of the structures can be studied. Moreover, contemplating them from more distant viewpoints, reached by stimulating walks over the open fellsides, one can appreciate the task that John Crossley, the engineer-in-chief of the Midland Railway, had in finding a way through. In F.S. Williams classic work, *The Midland Railway; Its rise and progress*, published in 1876, the outstanding features of the Settle and Carlisle line are splendidly dramatised in many contemporary engravings; and it is good to record that all the great structures stand today, four-square to the worst weather that wild region can produce, as when they were first built, now more than 100 years ago.

Chapter 9

Artistry in concrete

By the turn of the century the railway network of Great Britain was nearly complete. Nevertheless, in the same year that the West Highland Railway was opened to Fort William, 1894, an extension to the west coast was authorised. It was, as a writer in *The Railway Magazine* commented, on the completion of that extension, in 1901, 'one of those very rare cases in which the electric spark of a common interest flashes between the positive element of commercial advantage and the negative element of philanthropic undertaking'. The Government of the day, realising the importance of the railway, went so far as to guarantee a dividend of three per cent, upon £260,000, which was about half the capital required for the construction of the line, and the first sod was cut in January 1897. It was realised from the outset that one of the major difficulties in the construction of the line would be the maintenance of the labour force at full strength. In a rugged, sparsely populated countryside, remote from all the amenities of modern life, work on a railway contract, however well paid, would not be attractive.

The engineering work, bridging, embankment and excavation was likely to be heavy; and, although an ample supply of material for bridge-building was likely to be available from that taken out of the cuttings, the likelihood of getting first class stone masons in such an area was as remote as the district itself. It was this situation among others that determined the use of concrete rather than conventional masonry work for all the bridges. Another factor was that the local stone, although extremely hard, was virtually unworkable. But what practically clinched the matter was that the firm of Robert McAlpine & Sons secured the contract for the building of the line. The head of that firm, now world renowned, Robert McAlpine, was known in civil engineering circles as 'Concrete Bob'. He was one of the first to make extensive use of what was then a relatively new building material, mass concrete, and conditions on the Mallaig extension of the West Highland Railway were almost ideal for it. The rock excavated from the cuttings, though too hard to be worked into blocks for ordinary masonry use could be crushed small; and, mixed with the best quality cement, it made a first class and relatively cheap building material. McAlpine's greatest difficulty was in attracting good carpenters, because the timber framework of the arches required first class shuttering, usually in difficult and inhospitable geographical conditions.

Rather more than 40 years ago I made by bicycle what could be called a concrete viaduct pilgrimage from Fort William to Mallaig. In years to come that railway 'road to the Isles' may well become more supremely historic than it is today, as a chain of monuments in mass-concrete likely to survive as the oldest in the world, in that medium; and a monument no less to Robert McAlpine. In its sublime grandeur of scenery the Mallaig Extension could, in some ways, be regarded as analogous to the Settle and Carlisle line, in that the tremendous mountain terrain demanded stupendous railway engineering works; but actually the analogy is no more than slight. The Settle and Carlisle was built, almost regardless of expense, as a heavy express main line; the 'Mallaig Road' was a case of blasting through a single line—a tenuous line of communication—as cheaply as possible. A Canadian railway littérateur once described the land west of Fort William as 'an outstandingly harsh piece of country'. One might describe as 'harsh' the opposition nature afforded to the men who were trying to build a railway through it, but I always find it astonishingly beautiful, and a glorious setting for the engineering and architectural works it contains.

It so happened that the pilgrimage by bicycle was not my first introduction to the line. I came to Mallaig first by the Macbrayne mail steamer from the Kyle of Lochalsh and, after a few short excursions, travelled southwards to Edinburgh by train. So I saw the greatest of the concrete viaducts, that across Glenfinnan, last, as a supreme climax to the journey! But if (as most visitors to the line do) one is travelling westwards from Fort William, and emerging from one of the many rock cuttings, there bursts upon one the great sweep of the railway across Glenfinnan with the breathtaking sight of the great curving viaduct. Travelling by train, however, on a line that is constantly twisting and turning, the vista is gone all too soon, and I like to recall calm days in late summer when I clambered up among the heather and looked down at a creation 'so delicate', as a noted Scots writer once expressed it, 'that the fairies might have built it'. Twenty-one arches ranged round a graceful curve, and set in a panorama of great mountains.

Technically, Glenfinnan viaduct is 1,248 feet long, and 100 feet high. The arches are all semi-circular, and of 50 foot-span. The piers, excepting Nos 8 and 13 are 20 feet long and 6 feet thick at the top; the remaining two are more massive, being 21 feet long and 15 feet thick at the top. The railway is on a curve

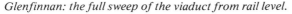

Glenfinnan: the full sweep of the viaduct from rail level.

Glenfinnan: an appreciation of the design and construction work in such a remote location comes from a study of this picture.

of 12 chains radius (960 feet) across the viaduct, and in section the piers are tapered so that the span of the arches is uniformly 50 feet at the inside and outside of the curve as well as on the centre line. From whatever angle one regards it the viaduct is tremendously impressive. Photographs taken when it was new show it standing out startlingly white against the dark hillsides, and a writer in *The Railway Magazine* of more than 70 years recalls that a great outcry was raised at the time at what he called 'the desecration of so historic and beautiful a spot as Glenfinnan by so ugly and commonplace a structure as a railway viaduct'. But knowing some of the remoter glens to north and south of the line, and how infrequently they are visited, even today, one wonders how many visitors would ever have come to know Glenfinnan also if it had *not* been for the railway. And, of course, with the weathering of the concrete the viaduct very quickly blended into complete harmony with the majestic scenery.

The next concrete viaduct of any magnitude is at Loch nan Uamh (in pronunciation the final mh is silent). On the railway, in both directions of travel, it is approached and crossed so suddenly that one is scarcely aware of a viaduct at all—just a fleeting glimpse of this beautiful sea-loch, where Prince Charles Edward Stuart first set foot on Scottish soil in 1745, and whence he also made his hair's breadth escape in a French frigate, a year later. Seen from the sea, Robert McAlpine's viaduct forms a very picturesque, though by no means dominating, centre piece to the mountains so finely grouped round the head of the loch. On the western side the railway dives immediately into a tunnel cut in the solid rock. The scene, including the beautifully weathered concrete viaduct, is pleasing enough for that great Scottish landscape painter, Sir D.Y. Cameron, to have included it in the series of splendid drawings with which he illustrated Seton Gordon's book, *Highways and Byways in the West Highlands*.

From the viaduct the line immediately begins climbing on a very steep gradient of 1 in 48, and having swung round a full right angle to the left there are occasional glimpses through the trees of the head of the loch, and the viaduct. But by this time the train is nearing perhaps the most noteworthy of all the concrete structures on the line, once again a work of which the passenger

Opposite *Glenfinnan: the train from Mallaig, coming off the viaduct.* **Above** *Another striking West Highland viaduct: Loch nan Uamh.*

must necessarily remain almost completely oblivious. Immediately beyond the longest tunnel on the 'Mallaig Road', one of 350 yards, the line crosses the deep ravine in which flows the Borrodale Burn. The laird in these regions was A. Nicholson, of Arisaig House and, paying full regard to the susceptibilities of these wealthy and influential landowners, McAlpine approached him with a view to constructing an arched viaduct with piers extending down to burn level. Nicholson agreed provided that the piers were clad in granite. This was an expense that could not be accepted, and so the bold step was taken to bridge the ravine with a single-span concrete viaduct.

Shades of Brunel at Maidenhead! The Borrodale bridge has a clear span of 127 feet 6 inches with a rise of only 22 feet 6 inches. Never before had a mass-concrete span of such magnitude been built, and it attracted world-wide attention. To indicate something of its pioneer character, it was recorded afterwards that in the five years before Borrodale was completed only five other concrete bridges had been erected, *anywhere in the world*, and all of those were to carry the relatively light road traffic of the day. Today Borrodale lies deep in the woods of the Arisaig House lands and, while not exactly needing an archaeological 'dig', one certainly has to make a way through the trees to get a glimpse of it, other than walking along the railway. It carries the big modern diesel locomotives as surely as it has done successive generations of steam.

The last of the notable mass-concrete viaducts on the 'Mallaig Road' is in another difficult geographical location, where the waters of the immensely deep freshwater Loch Morar flow over magnificent falls, and then in a relatively narrow ravine debouch into a very pretty bay famed for its dazzling white sands. But picturesque scenery does not usually help the railway engineer, and here McAlpine built a 90-foot span over the River Morar with two smaller spans on the northern side. This viaduct, like Glenfinnan and Loch nan Uamh, is still in full view, and its fine proportions can be studied at leisure. The Mallaig

Extension, like the West Highland Railway itself, was operated from the outset by the North British Railway, and was fully absorbed into the larger system in 1908. It is good that it remains fully operational today. It would be interesting to know if any of those five predecessors of the Borrodale Burn bridge survive, or if, in the course of time, it has become the oldest surviving mass-concrete bridge in the world. The way to see them best is undoubtedly by road, as I did first; and fortunately the road (A830) is nowadays in much better shape than when I first rode over it and when the late Harry Batsford, in his book with Charles Fry *The Face of Scotland* (1933) described it as 'medieval in its surface as in its writhings'!

Thirty years after the Mallaig Extension of the West Highland Railway was brought into service there was another very interesting use of concrete for railway viaducts, which, so far as the labour force was concerned, had some points of striking similarity—this time in Northern Ireland. The former Belfast and Northern Counties Railway, by then the Northern Counties Committee section of the London Midland and Scottish, had a very awkward track layout on its main line from Belfast to the north and west. While the line to Carrickfergus and Larne Harbour ran by the western shore of Belfast Lough, trains for Antrim, Portrush and Londonderry ran on this coastal line as far as Greenisland, $6\frac{3}{4}$ miles, and then reversed direction and climbed on to the high ground traversed by the principal main line. That it was a time-consuming and expensive process had been realised for very many years. Indeed, as long previously as the year 1872 Parliamentary powers had been obtained to construct a direct line; but because of the high cost the work was not then undertaken. In 1930, however, the NCC section of the LMS had, in Major M.S. Speir, a manager of outstanding energy and drive, who was anxious to make radical improvements in the train service to the north coast and, with the Government of Northern Ireland equally anxious that works for the relief of unemployment should be undertaken, the opportunity to improve the junction layouts in the neighbourhood was then grasped.

As one of the main objects of the scheme was to provide employment the large viaducts that were required on the new direct line, and in the diversion of

The location of the beautiful concrete viaducts at Greenisland, Northern Ireland.

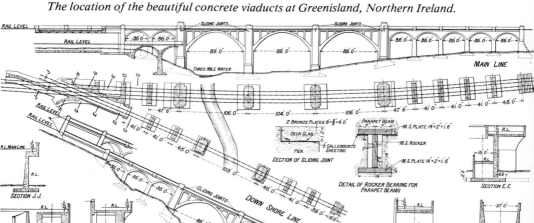

the down track on the shore line, were designed so that by far the greater part of the work could be done with direct labour, recruited from the local Labour Exchanges. Reinforced concrete was the natural medium for such a project, and an immense amount of highly skilled design and constructional planning was necessary to ensure that the work could be carried out safely and expeditiously with the largely unskilled and inexperienced labour that would be recruited specially to do the job. But there was nothing of a makeshift or amateurish nature about the viaducts as finished. They had a massive and imposing appearance, and were, of course, built to carry the standard loads specified for heavy main line railway traffic in Great Britain. At the time of their completion a technical description in one of the leading engineering journals referred to them as the largest of their kind carrying a railway in the British Isles. So far as the open arch form of construction was concerned, with open cross walls, this was certainly true, but in their maximum span of 89 feet, they were slightly surpassed by the largest span of McAlpine's Morar viaduct on the Mallaig line, and handsomely by the tremendous 127 foot 6 inch span of the Borrodale Burn bridge.

Dimensions apart, however, the Greenisland viaducts are a splendid, and most attractive looking job. How the actual finish of the surfaces was obtained is interesting. All the concreting material was obtained locally and it was consolidated behind the shuttering, partly by hand and partly by vibratory tools. A novel method of varying the shuttering was used whereby the finished face of the concrete, which was untouched, presented a variegated and attractive appearance. No money was available for an elaborate treatment of the surface, and it was decided to leave the concrete just as it came from the forms with the board marks visible. This gave the necessary finished effect. I shall not forget one winter's occasion when I saw the viaducts in unusual circumstances. In the course of a number of business visits to Belfast and the NCC line, I had become familiar with them and how their construction had come to invert the old process of directional reversal at Greenisland. On one occasion, when intending to take the day service from Portrush to London, via

Greenisland: deep snow adds an additional beauty to the double-tracked main line viaduct.

France: a spectacular recent example at Longeray sur le Rhône, built in replacement of a viaduct destroyed in the Second World War.

Larne, Stranraer and Carlisle, I had been concerned to see that there was no more than a five-minute connection in Belfast between the arrival of the Portrush train and the departure of the Larne boat express. Supposing we were late and missed the connection?

I need not have worried. Major Speir was as faultless an operator as he was a general manager. The same set of coaches did both jobs. I remember the exhilaration of riding down the 1 in 75 gradient of the main Greenisland viaducts at top speed, on the engine of the North Atlantic Express; having little more time than to walk smartly from one end of the train to the other in the Belfast terminus, mount the fresh engine and then go storming out for Larne to dive under that viaduct little more than 20 minutes later, on the single tracked viaduct of the down shore line. That was all at the start of a benign summer day; but things were very different when the steamer from Heysham arrived before breakfast time one February morning to find Belfast under about six inches of snow. When I checked in at the railway offices 'The Major', as we all called him, conceded that I had come over on rather a bad day; but there was work to be done at the junctions, and I took a local train out to Jordanstown station, on the shore line just beyond the viaducts. Under their canopy of deep snow these stately structures looked incredibly beautiful. In years to come, when they become increasingly revered as monuments of great distinction, it is to be hoped that the circumstances of their construction will not be forgotten. They were designed by William Kelly Wallace, who in later years crossed the water to become Chief Civil Engineer of the LMS.

Chapter 10

Monumental old signal boxes

The evolution of railway signalling practice, from the early adaptation of the old Admiralty semaphores with stirrup actuation, and large manual levers, to the highly sophisticated solid-state electronic technology of today, would need not one but many entire books to deal with it comprehensively; and I am making no attempt to produce even a 'potted' version just now. But the buildings in which the regulating apparatus was housed, modestly called boxes, provide a wide field for investigation for those who seek, by searching out old drawings and photographs to build up a picture of what railway operation was like, a hundred years ago, or more. Of the various structures, to be described in this chapter few physical traces of them remain. One is almost entirely dependent upon old documents.

In tracing things back to the very beginnings a modern researcher might feel that the pioneer railway managements had little regard for the health and general well-being of the men concerned with actually running the trains. For many years after the epoch-marking trials at Rainhill the locomotives had no shelter whatever for the driver and fireman, and it was the same with the earliest equipment for working signals and points. It must be remembered, however, that in the 1830s we were only just beginning to move away from the days of the stage coaches, and the drivers and guards of those conveyances had no protection from the weather. There is one recorded instance of a humanitarian designer who put a shelter round the footplate of a new type of locomotive, and received a petition from the men to take it off, because they could not see!

It was C.H. Gregory, afterwards Sir Charles Gregory, who installed what could be claimed as the father of all signal boxes at Bricklayers Arms Junction, Bermondsey, in 1843, on the London and Croydon Railway. Semaphores, generally of the Admiralty type, had already been used for controlling train movements in a general sense, but the major step taken by Gregory was to group all the masts for the semaphores relating to this junction in one place, and mount the stirrups by which the signalman actuated them on a single frame. To give the man a better view of the traffic the frame was mounted on an elevated platform. Even so, the whole affair was entirely in the open, with no shelter of any kind for the man in charge of it. For this reason it was sometimes referred to as a 'signal station', and it was interesting to find this name surviving in some instances, when much larger and more sophisticated apparatus, in totally enclosed cabins, was involved, more than 50 years later. The open platform survived for little more than ten years after Gregory's pioneer installation at

Bricklayers Arms Junction, and it was John Saxby's developments, while still
working as a blacksmith in the locomotive works at Brighton, that led the way
towards the earliest form of signal 'box'.

These were extraordinarily picturesque affairs. The operating platform was
about 10 to 12 feet above rail level, and the 'frame' containing the levers,
included all those necessary for actuating the neighbouring group of points and
signals at a junction. How Saxby interlocked the signal and point levers so that
the position of these corresponded, and made for safe working of the trains, is
apart from present considerations. A wooden shelter, with opening windows all
the way round was built on to the operating platform, but the most
distinguished feature of these very first signal boxes was that the semaphore
signals themselves were carried on masts sprouting out of the roofs. An
interesting point in operating was thereby involved. The signals were there to
instruct drivers when to stop and where to proceed but, displayed in a composite
group high above the signal box roof, they did not tell a driver *where* he should
stop, nor did it appear very obvious which of the various semaphores he should
heed. The driver had to know, from his familiarity with the track layout, which
was his signal and, if it was at danger, where to stop. If going too far might
involve his fouling the intersection of another line, and running the risk of a
collision, it was left to his judgment to stop clear of the fouling point concerned.

In a busy station yard, such as Brighton itself, there would be several of these
quaint old signal boxes dotted about the area, all with their distinguishing nests
of signal masts. The semaphores all had lamps for providing coloured light
indications at night, and several tiers of landings and access ladders were built
into the structure for the men who had to tend the lamps. Those old signal boxes
did not lack picturesque names. There was one on the outskirts of Brighton
called 'Lover's Walk', and another at St Leonards named 'Bo-peep Junction'.
Perhaps the most famous of all those installed by the firm of Saxby and Farmer,
known by reputation rather than actual experience for most people, was
Stewarts Lane Junction, Battersea, also on the London Brighton and South
Coast Railway, and controlling the junction where the broad-gauge trains of the
Great Western came on to the Brighton line in the approach to the Victoria
terminus, in Pimlico. It was because Saxby and Farmer used a picture of this
box in their registered trade mark that it became so well known, though it is
likely that few who knew that trade mark knew where or what the installation
was. The 'cabin' had to be carried unusually high on the 'stilts' in order that the
signalman could see over the intervening line of the London and South Western
Railway. There were mixed gauge tracks in the foreground to carry the broad
gauge trains of the Great Western Railway.

A close scrutiny of the apparatus on those masts above the signal box roof
shows that there is apparently only one lamp associated with each of two
semaphores pointing in either direction. That lamp was a masterpiece of
ingenuity, because it was designed to display lights corresponding to the
position of *both* semaphore arms. Inside the fixed case, which had clear glass
lenses pointing in each direction, there were two revolving tables; these were
attached severally to half-cranks operated by the signal down rods. The upper
crank was attached to a hollow vertical shaft, which formed a sleeve over the
shaft for the lower crank. Each of the tables had its own red and green glass
and, according to whether the semaphore arm was 'on' or 'off', the appropriate
coloured glass was moved between the central paraffin oil lamp (with glass

Above *Stewart's Lane Junction, Battersea: a characteristic example of a very early form of signal box, with the posts carrying the semaphores on top of the box. (An illustration from* Saxby & Farmer's Railway Safety Appliances, *1905).* **Below** *A highly spectacular example of the early Saxby form of signal box in the approach to London Bridge in the 1860s.*

chimney) and the clear lens in the outer casing. This fascinating lamp was a standard product of Saxby & Farmer for very many years.

One of the most unusual of the early signal 'boxes' was that at the entrance to Victoria Station, the 'Hole in the Wall'. The original terminus of the Brighton Railway and its administrative headquarters, until it became part of the Southern Railway, in 1923, was at London Bridge, and its penetration into the West End began in 1856, with its securing working rights of a small railway with the high sounding name of West End of London & Crystal Palace Junction. This took them to the south bank of the Thames, at Battersea, and then came the Victoria Station and Pimlico Railway, of which the bridge across the river was opened in 1858. Originally there were only two tracks into Victoria station, which the Brighton had to share with the London Chatham and Dover, and the Great Western, from 1861 onwards; and it was to control the entrance to the station area, half of which was leased to the other two companies, that the Brighton put in the 'Hole in the Wall' signal 'box'. It was located so that the signalmen had a view into the Brighton side of the terminus, a layout of which, it was once said, every line crossed every other; but the view into the Chatham side was partially obscured. It contained no more than 18 full-sized levers, and four smaller ones in what seems to have been a subsidiary frame, but it was considered quite a wonderful piece of work. It was open at the front, though protected from the weather by a glass roof that covered this bottleneck approach to the terminal station.

The need to provide signalmen with the widest possible views over all the passing traffic led to the practice of siting signal boxes on gantries spanning all the tracks, at the entrance to large stations. The viaduct leading across the Thames into the terminus of the South Eastern Railway at Charing Cross, had abutments on the City side, crowned with some highly ornamental stonework, and each with a spectacular array of five huge gaslamps. Crossing the four

Below left *The first box and signals in the approach to Waterloo.* **Above** *The 'Hole in the Wall' box at Victoria, Brighton line.* **Below** *A very old photograph showing, on the right, the location of the 'Hole in the Wall', at a time when mixed gauge track was laid into this station to permit entry by Great Western broad gauge trains.*

tracks on the bridge was a lattice girder structure carrying the signal box, from the roof of which there were three masts, each carrying two of the twin-semaphore type of Saxby and Farmer signals. The operating rods for these signals were taken conveniently upwards through the roof of the box, while the rods for working the many points in the approaches and in the station itself were neatly ensconced in wide recesses in those massive bridge abutments. The ensemble made a most imposing entry to the station, albeit only one that could be seen to advantage by the engine driver! The companion South Eastern terminus, at Cannon Street, was equipped on similar, but more elaborate lines because there were many more platforms in the station, and six tracks across the bridge. The signal box had four masts rising from its roof and all of these carried four sets of semaphores, one above the other. Not all these were of the twin-arm type, but there were enough of them in all conscience, and the sheer height of this edifice required no fewer than three access galleries, one above the other, for servicing the lamps and oiling the mechanisms. The uppermost semaphore arms must have been a full 70 feet above rail level—and that out on the bridge over the Thames! The point that always comes to mind, and which I have never seen satisfactorily answered, is how they managed in the thick of a 'London Particular'!

As the intensity of railway working increased, and safety requirements compelled the use of more elaborate signalling, the number and the location of individual boxes became a matter of growing concern. At a great junction complex like York, for example, there had to be a number of boxes, each dealing with a particular facet of the working, yet linked together by slotting of the actual signal mechanisms in some cases, and by audible co-ordination by telephone and block instrument links in others. While this is, briefly, bringing matters forward to the turn of the century, the situation at York may be mentioned as indicating how things had then developed. At the south end there was Locomotive Yard Box, with 129 levers, covering the southern approaches. At the north end there were two boxes facing each other, on either side of the main line, one dealing with northbound and another, southbound traffic, while

Charing Cross: after the widening of the bridge over the Thames and enlargement of the station, about 1900.

Maidenhead Bridge: a Great Western signal box in the days of the broad gauge (British Railways).

in the centre of the station, the co-ordinating point for the whole working was the Central box. Between them the four boxes had 391 levers. These four boxes remained until the great resignalling, with colour lights, was brought into service in 1951. The building that housed the one-time 'Central' box, afterwards renamed 'Platform', still remains today, though no longer as a signal box. It is a very attractively styled building at the eastern end of the main footbridge in the middle of the station.

The need to locate signal boxes so that the movement of trains was under the constant scrutiny of signalmen led to some curious and perhaps uncongenial places of work for the men. This was a situation that was entirely eliminated with the gradual introduction of track circuiting in the early years of the 20th century, because then the movement of a train could be watched by the indicating lights on an illuminated track diagram. Before the coming of track circuiting, and of electric traction, one of the most grisly locations for a signal box was to be found on the Inner Circle line in London. Half-way between the stations Edgware Road and Paddington (Praed Street) is the junction where the Hammersmith and City line joins. It is the connection to the Great Western main line, and when I was commuting from Ealing to Kings Cross some 50 years ago there were through trains. The junction is entirely in tunnel, and in steam days there had to be a signal box alongside, in a hole excavated beside the tracks. There are, of course, many control centres on the London Underground system that are entirely underground, but none immediately adjacent to an all-steam line, a line moreover carrying a very heavy traffic.

Out in the open, and apart from the rather special designs of signal box suited to the larger junctions and terminal stations, the buildings erected at the smaller stations showed a remarkable variety of designs. In the days before the grouping of the main line railways in 1923, if one came to a line in unfamiliar country the connoisseur could usually tell to what company it belonged by the constructional style of the signal boxes. That style was by no means dictated by economic conditions. Some of the railways paying the highest dividends to their shareholders had standardised on very simple, light, if not necessarily flimsy structures, while others, not so affluent, built signal boxes that looked as if they were designed to withstand a siege! Climatic conditions did not seem to enter into it either, because the Highland Railway, maybe in that case for economic reasons, used a fairly light all-timber design. Once the need for a properly covered in 'box' was generally recognised, certain modest amenities were included in the equipment, such as oil heating stoves, and means for boiling kettles or cooking meals. The manning of country signal boxes, in which the man was alone for eight or ten hours, and required at all times to be alert to the last degree, was a very lonely job.

While all-timber signal boxes tended to be confined to smaller interlockings, there were some spectacular survivals of earlier days. When the first Saxby equipment was put in on the Brighton main line, around 1860, there was a remarkable example of the much-elevated type of cabin at Folly Hill, near Haywards Heath. It originally had the signal posts extended through the roof but, at a later time, the signals themselves were arranged in their appropriate positions adjacent to the track, and one of the standard Saxby interlocking frames substituted for the stirrup type. But the cabin remained, sky-high, carried on four massive stilts, 15 feet high, and reached by a double-tier stairway from ground level. But on several of the British railways the high-elevated all-timber cabin was by no means an archaic survival. The Lancashire and Yorkshire had many of them, carried not upon timber stilts but on massive steel frameworks. The signal manufacturers of late Victorian times developed their own styles of cabin construction, because it was their part of a contract that the supply and erection of the signal box should be included. When I joined Westinghouse, in 1925, the carpenters shop was one of the largest in the factory at Chippenham.

Many railways used a hybrid design of signal box, with the ground floor encased in brick or stone, and everything above the operating floor in timber. The signal contractors developed this type also, though the building of the lower portion on site had to be sub-contracted. This became the most usual form of small and medium-sized boxes in mechanical signalling days. When the amenity of a stove for heating or cooking was added, the chimney was built in brick, or stone, for obvious reasons! As the practice of railway signalling became more sophisticated, and the ground floors of cabins came to include electrical apparatus, in addition to the interlocking mechanism for the levers, an increased degree of protection was necessary. At the time of the Second World War, when many hundreds of signal boxes of this type were still in use, the windows were bricked up as a protection against flying debris in air raids. Upstairs, however, the signalman had still to see out, and with glass all round him many of them must have felt very uncomfortable at times.

Some railways, notably the Great Eastern and the Great Northern, did not seem to adopt a completely standard type of signal box, even for installations made in the early years of the 20th century. Both had many all-wood and all-brick examples and even the Great Western, which in its all-brick design became

Opposite page top *A quaint old signal box at Dover that survived until the construction of the new Marine station.* **Centre** *Waterloo: the box across the tracks and the tremendous array of semaphores, 1895.* **Bottom** *A typical example of an elevated box from the North Eastern Railway.*

ADMIRALTY PIER. DOVER.

An elegant timber cabin, Manchester, Lancashire and Yorkshire Railway.

perhaps more nearly standard than the majority of the British railways in the pre-grouping era, had its own peculiarities, when questions of giving the signalman an uninterrupted view of traffic movements arose. One of the most extraordinary was at my present home station, Bath Spa. The old Brunellian station, with its picturesque all-over roof, had long since been modified, and the relatively sharp curves at each end leading to the straight platform roads altered to give a continuous sweeping curve, albeit one always subject to a speed limit of 30 mph for non-stopping trains. To give a comprehensive outlook on the workings at both ends of the station a wooden signal box was erected on the top of the awning of the down platform. Viewing it from the up platform it looked as though that box had no support, other than the awning itself, until one crossed over to the down side, and saw the massive girders that were, almost surreptitiously, carried out from Brunel's original station wall. All the point rodding, and wires for signal operation were carried down to rail level in a channel in the station wall suitably occult from public view.

Another unusual and highly picturesque signal box, near an earlier home of mine, was at Millwood Junction on the Furness Railway. When this railway was first projected Barrow itself was little more than a village, and the prime purpose was to convey iron ore from Kirkby and Askam to Piel Pier, for shipment across Morecambe Bay. The town of Dalton-in-Furness was at the end of a short branch reached by the spur now traversed by the steam-hauled Cumbrian Coast Express. Later, when the direct connection from the east to Barrow was laid in, Millwood Junction became the third of a group of junctions in the area. But with the opening of the direct line through Barrow to the north the original link from Askam fell into disuse and, by the time of the First World War, the track had been lifted. Though no longer a junction the signal box was still in operation in 1919, though merely forming an intermediate block post between Furness Abbey and Dalton Junction. Quite apart from its history, however, it was the box itself that remains a memory. To my lasting regret I never photographed it.

Partly concealed, except from the line itself, amid the trees that grew up the side of that fair vale in which Furness Abbey is ensconced—so strangely named 'The Valley of Deadly Nightshade'—it stood tall and brooding, more like some medieval watch-tower on the Rhine than an English railway signal box. As a teenager with a Box-Brownie camera I remember climbing down among the trees, and chatting up the old signalman; but in my then-obsession with locomotives I was more concerned with trains on the way than of that priceless old signal box.

It had an almost exact twin on the right bank of the River Dee, near its mouth, containing the hydraulic power equipment for operating the tremendous Hawarden Swing Bridge, with its 170-foot span, carrying the line of the former Manchester, Sheffield and Lincolnshire Railway into North Wales. It was not a signal box in the ordinary sense, though the levers in it controlling the hydraulic actuating gear for the bridge were electrically interlocked with the railway block working between the signal boxes on either side. Hawarden bridge attracted much attention at the time of its construction in 1890, because it was then the largest opening bridge in the world.

Chapter 11

Early interlocking frames— some marvels of mechanical contrivance

Over the years many travellers will have had glimpses of the operating floor of a signal box, and seen the long row of mechanical levers, dressed with the precision of guardsmen on parade, with a cloth always ready to hand, so that the signalman, when pulling them, did not have to touch those glittering handles, so lovingly burnished. Many of the old signal boxes were within sight of any interested party on the station platforms, but the levers, painted in distinguishing colours according to their various functions, were actually no more than the façade. The heart and soul of the job, the interlocking that safeguarded the entire operation, was either below floors, or in sealed containers. Few outsiders were privileged to enter the 'holy of holies' below the operating floor—even the signalmen themselves. The integrity of the interlocking was the rock-bottom foundation of safe working, and in ordinary circumstances it was only the maintenance men, under the invigilating eye of a signal inspector, who had access to the locking. How the vital safeguards were effected was a matter of great diversity among the various manufacturers of signalling equipment, and equally among those railway companies like the London and North Western, and the Great Western, who manufactured their own. But having mentioned the levers and their colours, before going downstairs, as it were, the distinctive colours can be recalled.

The standard colours in use for many years were: signals (except 'distants')— red; points—black; facing point locks—blue; spare levers—white and gate stops—brown. The levers of distant signals, giving warning of the approach to a signal, at which a stop was obligatory if it was in the danger position, were originally green; but in the mid-1920s these were changed to yellow. Contemporaneously with this change, the levers for warning gongs, used in some localities at level crossings, were changed from yellow to green. These colours were not used everywhere on British railways in pre-grouping days. For example, some companies did not distinguish their distant signal levers by special colours, while special functions that might be found in isolated locations had colour codes of their own. Nevertheless the five listed at the beginning of this paragraph were standard as between most railways.

To appreciate the diversity and complexity that developed in the design and construction of interlocking frames the basic principles of interlocking must be defined. They did not constitute a code of practice that was postulated at one stroke. It was gradually evolved over a period of many years, as experience in operating railways accumulated, and accidents revealed shortcomings both in the developing principles, and in the apparatus. The fundamental factor to be observed, in all cases, is that a signal must not be cleared to permit a train to proceed until the points are correctly set; and that once the signal concerned is cleared it must be physically impossible for the signalman to set up another route that would intersect the first, and so set up, what is referred to in modern popular parlance as a 'collision course'. In referring to the colours of levers I referred to the distant signal. The interlocking must prevent the lever for this being pulled until all the associated signals under the control of the signal box are cleared.

At an early stage in the history of railways in Great Britain the Inspecting Officers of the Board of Trade were active in requiring safety features to be added to the equipment—not always to the liking of the railway managements, who always had an eye towards the expense of extra mechanical features. There was a classic early instance of the perspicacity of the Board of Trade Inspectorate in 1860 when Colonel Yolland was making his examination of the signalling at Kentish Town Junction. The signals were lowered by the signalman putting his foot into a stirrup, and then pressing down, and the engineer responsible had contrived a simple interlock so that when the signal for the main line was lowered you could not move the signal for the branch line. On the face of it there could be no confusion from this source. But having had this demonstrated to him Colonel Yolland stepped forward, carefully manoeuvred his foot so that it was astride both stirrups, pressed down, and lowered both signals at once! The engineer had to try again; but although it could be argued that no signalman would ever attempt to do what the Colonel had successfully accomplished, the fact that it was possible to fool the mechanism had been demonstrated made it necessary to guard against it. It must never be forgotten that mistakes in signalling can cause fatal accidents.

While railway managements were apt to resist the imposing upon them of safety requirements, on the grounds of expense, a new breed of mechanical inventors was born, paying careful heed to the features recommended by the Inspecting Officers of the Board of Trade, and designing apparatus for which they immediately sought patent protection. These ingenious and far-seeing men saw, what some of the more obstinate of the railway managers sought to forestall, the day when interlocking apparatus would be required at every station and every junction in the country. The field seemed boundless, and the prospects for good business infinite. Furthermore, even in the somewhat primitive state of the art that had been attained by the 1860s, Great Britain was well ahead of Continental countries, and the prospects were attractive even beyond Europe. Extraordinary ingenuity was shown by the rival manufacturers. It had to be, because the field was becoming so congested that one had to design something different from everyone else, or go out of business. It was as simple as that!

In February 1934, Ralph S. Griffiths was elected President of the Institution of Railway Signal Engineers, and for the subject of his Presidential Address he chose the development of the interlocking frame. Beginning with the primitive stirrup actuation of the 1840s, by the time he had traced the story forward another 50 years, he had described and illustrated some 40 different types of apparatus—virtually 40 different ways of doing the same job! Out of this amazing 'free-for-all' there emerged at first three major competitors: Stevens and Sons, Saxby and Farmer, and McKenzie and Holland—to be joined, towards the end of the 19th century by Dutton and Co, and just at the turn by Evans O'Donnell. Saxby had a formidable competitor in Easterbrook, with both inventors trying to establish a patent right to the principle of actuating the locking by means of the lever catch handle. This principle is explained later; but the cost of the litigation bore heavily on Easterbrook and, after a lengthy action following the introduction of his 1868 apparatus, he dropped out of the picture.

This patent case had a surprising and fascinating turn for me in 1940, of all unlikely years. In the Westinghouse works at Chippenham every square yard of space was needed for wartime production, and obsolete equipment, and other impedimenta was being scrapped relentlessly, to make more room. My attention was drawn to some models that had been used for demonstration layouts, and among them was a one-eighth full size model of a 20-lever interlocking frame. Greatly intrigued, I obtained permission to rescue this from the impending scrap heap, and having set it up—rusted solid as it was—in the garage of my wartime home, I was exceedingly puzzled. It was not any one of the various types of Saxby, or McKenzie frame. At the first opportunity I looked out my copy of *Griffith's Presidential Address*, and then I had no difficulty in identifying it as an Easterbrook 1868 pattern frame. But why Easterbrook? It was not likely that Saxby and Farmer would have made so beautiful and accurate a model for demonstration, of a deadly rival apparatus, unless—? Was it an exhibit, in the patent case that finally put Easterbrook out of business? I suppose the origin of that model will now never be known.

When the Inspecting Officers of the Board of Trade began asking for some positive interlock to be provided between levers to prevent wrong routes, or 'collision courses' to be set up inadvertently, there was considerable variation in the way inventors set out to do this, but the great milestone—perhaps the greatest of all in the history of signalling in its mechanical days—was the introduction by Stevens & Sons in 1870, of tappet locking. Like all great inventions, it was so simple: a tappet directly attached to each of the levers, having bevelled notches cut in it that drove the cross-locks. Although Stevens had no difficulty in securing the necessary patent protection for this, the simplest-ever of all means of actuation, it would appear that the company was

not very business-minded; because while they secured many important contracts, their rivals, producing much more complicated and expensive apparatus, secured many times more, by highly efficient marketing methods. In the United Kingdom the Stevens type of interlocking frame was more popular in Scotland than in England, and was extensively used on the Caledonian, the North British and on the Great North of Scotland. Farther south, the Furness Railway had some. The frames of the now-privately owned Lakeside and Haverthwaite Railway are of this type, but by far the largest user in England was the London and South Western.

Stevens used the principle known as 'direct-lever' locking. Although there was a catch handle on the lever this merely lifted the cast-iron 'drop-box' that registered the position of the lever on the quadrant plate in the full-normal, or full-reverse position. John Saxby, on the other hand, applied interlocking to the very initiation of the lever movement, in other words to the catch handle. If a lever had to be locked against a conflicting movement you could not even lift the catch, let alone pull the lever. Easterbrook did the same thing. But after these great, one-time rivals had fought it out in the law courts, and Stevens, in 1870, had patented his tappet locking, Saxby brought out his celebrated 'rocker' actuation. When, in 1874, he added the 'grid' form of locking he produced an apparatus that R.S. Griffiths in that notable Presidential Address described as: '. . . perhaps the greatest medium for arousing world-wide interest in British signalling practice. Frames of this design have been employed in nearly every country where railways exist'. It was a relatively complicated affair, but Saxby's marketing must have been superb, for it became standard in Belgium, on certain of the French railways and, above all, in the USA. In England it was most extensively used on the London Brighton and South Coast, Saxby's own railway. Today there are probably more examples of it surviving in the USA than anywhere else in the world, because there it remained standard for the longest time.

Despite its simplicity, the Stevens frame, with its direct lever locking, had the disadvantage that the stroke of the tappets was very long. The Worcester firm of McKenzie and Holland, while retaining the simplicity of lever, rather than

Left *The Stevens type of frame, here installed at South Bermondsey junction, London Brighton and South Coast Railway.*

Right *Saxby & Farmer's 'Rocker and Grid' type of interlocking frame from an article written by the author in* The Model Engineer, *April 11 1946.*

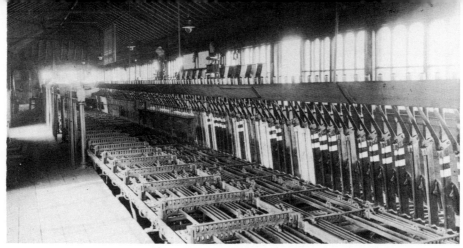

A very large Saxby 'Rocker and Grid' type frame at Brighton, London Brighton and South Coast Railway (Westinghouse Brake and Signal Co Ltd).

catch-handle locking, and thus steering clear of Saxby's patents (!), devised an ingenious form of cam actuation. The principle involved can be seen by reference to the drawing. On the lever is bolted a rectangular stud, normally resting in the notch marked (A): when the signalman attempts to pull the lever the stud presses against the face of the notch marked (C). Then, due to the oblique position of the cam pivot (B) the reaction between the stud and the surface (C) tends to turn the cam in a clockwise direction, and the stud becomes free to travel along the curved slot, which is now radial to the lever pivot. No further movement of the cam takes place until nearing the end of the lever stroke, when the stud reaches the stepped portion of the cam slot; then a further rotation of the cam is made. So, the tail of the cam, by which the locking is

McKenzie & Holland's 'Cam and Rocker' apparatus, again from an article by the author in The Model Engineer, *June 20 1946.*

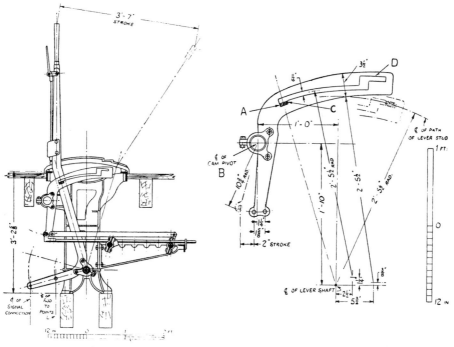

operated, is given a stroke of 1 inch during the first movement of the lever, and a further 1 inch at the end.

The locking was effected by a duplex action through two horizontal connections from the tail of the cam. One was a link that was attached at the opposite end to a rocker for oscillating the shafts running longitudinally, while the other was a tappet of triangular cross-section, which had notches cut in its flanges to engage with the projections of the locking dogs, which in their turn were rocked by the oscillating motion of the horizontal rods. It was a complicated business; but made with precision and skill interlocking machines of this kind worked extremely well, and lasted for very many years. A fine example at Leeds, Canal Box, on the former North Eastern Railway was not taken out of service until 1937; but McKenzie and Holland, through establishment of a subsidiary company in Melbourne, and another in Brisbane, secured a virtual monopoly of the Australian market, and I saw one of the 'cam and rocker' type of frames still in service at the great Flinders Street station at Melbourne in 1973.

Beautifully as these machines, by both Saxby and Farmer, and by McKenzie and Holland, were made, both firms swooped upon the very simple tappet locking principle initiated by Stevens & Sons, when, in 1887, that firm characteristically allowed their patent rights to lapse. McKenzie and Holland retained their cam action to provide a 2 inch stroke for the tappet, and their 'cam and tappet' frame became an even greater favourite than the preceding 'cam and rocker'. In the meantime Saxby and Farmer produced their duplex plunger type, in 1888, which has remained to this day a standard for mechanical working on the South African Railways. In Great Britain the Saxby '1888' never superseded the celebrated 'rocker and grid' of 1874, although it was a good deal cheaper. By that time most of the British railways were fully equipped with

The kind of track layout for which interlocking had to be provided: Newcastle, east end, North Eastern Railway.

A works photograph of a McKenzie & Holland 'Cam and Rocker' type frame, with hand wheel for locking level crossing gates—from an early brochure of theirs.

interlocking apparatus; and the products of the three principal manufacturers were so well made, and lasted so long, that replacements were necessary only when developing traffics required enlarged or altered station and junction layouts. The more lasting Saxby designs using tappet locking did not come until after the amalgamation with Evans O'Donnell & Co, of Chippenham in 1905.

In the meantime an interesting and significant event in signalling history must be recalled. In recognition of the large amount of business that would be involved in the signalling and interlocking of the largest of the British railways, the London and North Western, the partners John Saxby, and J.S. Farmer, had set up their works alongside its main line, at Kilburn, and the association between the company and the signalling manufacturers became close and profitable. Now Saxby was a very forceful character, and having obtained this advantageous foothold he proceeded to 'press his luck'. In 1867 the so-called 'spindle locking' apparatus had been introduced, and many frames were supplied to the LNWR and in 1871 came the first version of the famous 'rocker' actuation. Saxby felt that he was sufficiently well established for the new design to be accepted without question, but in that same year a very significant new appointment had been made: Francis W. Webb had succeeded John Ramsbottom, as Chief Mechanical Engineer.

This was not all. Ten years earlier Richard Moon had become Chairman of the LNWR, a man who for 30 years waged a ruthless campaign of cutting down expenditure—though never to the extent of skimping on the equipment of the line. He abhorred all agents, and 'middle-men', and urged his engineering officers never to use contractors if equipment could be made in the railway shops. His new mechanical engineer was as forceful a character as Saxby, and it was not long before they came into head-on collision. Webb was as prolific and versatile an inventor as any man then living, and as early as 1873 he was authorised by the Board of the LNWR to set up a complete manufactory in Crewe Works for all the signalling equipment the company needed. This, of course, included the production of an interlocking frame. It was not in Webb's nature to accept the design of an existing manufacturer, and build it under licence; he must design his own. The outcome was described in a paper read before the Institution of Civil Engineers by his signal superintendent, A.M. Thompson, in May 1885:

'The amount of wear and tear in a frame working a busy junction is so great, that, if badly constructed, it is sure to be frequently out of order, and at a time when perhaps it is almost impossible, on account of the traffic, to effect the necessary repairs. Mr. Webb, therefore, kept prominently in view the advantage of having a strong machine, of the simplest possible construction, few parts and these interchangeable, large wearing surfaces, and the whole easily accessible for cleaning and repairs; and he decided that it would be more economical in the end to fit it up with as much care as is bestowed upon a locomotive engine, relying on special machinery to cheapen production, rather than, as it were, to throw rough castings together without fitting, as had been too frequently the case. Somewhat hampered at the start by the claims of inventors, an apparatus was produced which embodied all the characteristics constituting a good machine.

'Instead of casting the quadrant-plate in one piece to contain from ten to fifteen levers, as is the usual practice, each lever is centred on a casting which forms its own quadrant, and these levers and quadrants are, so to speak, threaded together to form an apparatus of any desired size.'

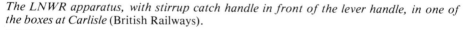

The LNWR apparatus, with stirrup catch handle in front of the lever handle, in one of the boxes at Carlisle (British Railways).

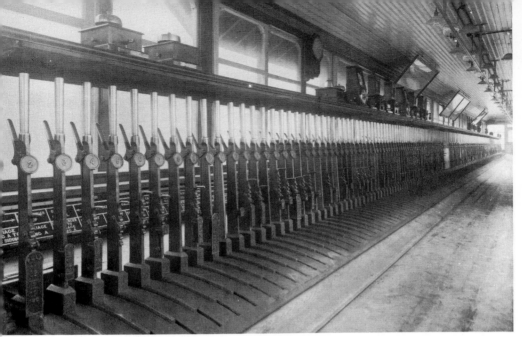

At the time of its installation, the largest mechanical interlocking frame in the world—260 levers in one row. This was on the North British Railway at Edinburgh, Waverley East End.

This later became standard practice on the interlocking frames of all manufacturers. But what was striking to an observer on the operating floor of any signal box on the London and North Western Railway, all of which were in due course fitted up with Webb's apparatus, was the design of the catch handle. Whether he did this to be different from everyone else, and thereby avoid patent rights is not clear, but it always looked a most awkward appliance. Webb used lever, rather than catch-handle locking, and the massive drop box that registered the position of the lever in its full normal or full reverse position was raised by a loop handle on the front of the lever, instead of by the conventional spring-loaded catch handle at the back of the lever. Thompson in his paper stated that this was a detail highly appreciated by the signalmen; but having to use one hand to push down the loop-handle, and then to pull the lever did not seem a very ergonomic operation, and no other railway, or manufacturer copied it. At the time of Thompson's paper (May 1885) there were already 13,250 levers of Webb's design in use on the LNWR and, by the turn of the century, an equal number had been installed in replacement of others of older design.

The description of Webb's interlocking frame really brings to an end the formative period in mechanical interlocking practice. With the expiring of the Stevens patent, and adoption by all manufacturers, including the London and North Western Railway, of the great principle of tappet locking, whether by direct or indirect lever actuation, or by catch handle, the scene was set for the 20th century developments leading eventually to the elimination of the positive mechanical 'lock', and its replacement first by an electro-mechanical appliance, and later by pure electric circuitry. But, however sophisticated the modern means of achievement may be, the underlying principles remain precisely those hammered out by the great pioneers of the 19th century—however primitive, however complicated their means of actuation may have been.

Chapter 12

Passenger travel of yesterday

In taking a leisurely walk round the majestically arranged National Railway Museum at York in search of visible reminders of what railway travel was like 150 years ago, the visitor, looking at the grand assemblage objectively, cannot fail to be struck by the heavy preponderance of locomotives to carriages among the full-sized exhibits. There is, of course, no doubt that the technical and emotive appeal of the steam locomotive is much greater than that of the coaching stock it hauled, and much more zeal has been shown in the preservation of historic locomotives. It is always noticeable that, on the increasing number of steam-hauled special trains run today in Great Britain, the vintage locomotives are usually hauling modern rolling stock. This, of course, is to some extent a sociological necessity since it would not be possible to provide the amenities of travel expected today in 'period' coaches even if they were available. So, reverting to the National Railway Museum, one finds the most spectacular examples of coaching stock are some of the 'specials' of a bygone age—Royal saloons, vintage dining cars, travelling post offices, and such like, rather than the ordinary carriages provided on the regular service trains.

Passengers were carried on the Stockton and Darlington Railway, but in the most unprepossessing, and dismally appointed wooden carts, drawn by horses, and it was not until the opening of the Liverpool and Manchester Railway in 1830 that the conveyance of passengers in large numbers became a major integral part of railway business. It was a development that was not looked upon with any great favour by the men whose lavish investment had made the railways possible. It was a time of much political unrest in Great Britain, of agitation for reform of the franchise, and a positive gulf in the economic situation between what have been called the 'Haves' and the 'Have-Nots'. Of the Prime Minister of the day, the great Duke of Wellington, it was said that having defeated Napoleon he thought of an English politically-incited mob with much disquiet. He was afraid that the building of railways would facilitate the moving or organised bands of trouble makers from one inflamatory area to another. While the new railways were required by law to provide for all kinds of travellers—they were common carriers, and had to take whatever business was offered—they did not provide any particular inducements for the very lowest orders.

One depends very much upon the artists of the day to show what travel was like in the first decade of railway operation. On the Liverpool and Manchester Railway first, second and third class passenger accommodation was provided, and at first, not only were the third class vehicles devoid of any protection from the weather, but so also were the 'seconds'. One is intrigued to see crowded gatherings of gentlemen almost without exception in tall, highly polished hats, and ladies in large floppy hats and handsome dresses in open trucks, immediately behind the engine—20 passengers in a short four-wheeled truck. The costumes of the day, with the ladies decked in crinolines, would have seemed highly unsuitable for railway travel; things are rather left to the imagination. In York, however, with that exquisite example of a medieval street in the Castle Museum, with the shops peopled by superbly modelled waxworks, one wonders if at some future time an open four-wheeled 'second', crowded with period travellers in waxworks might not form one of the exhibits. I am sure it would have a well-nigh priceless educational value.

First class passengers were, of course, very welcome and everything was done for their comfort. The coaches were designed like the road vehicles to which affluent patrons were accustomed, namely the stage coaches, or the still more exclusive and expensive mails. Luggage was loaded on to the roofs, to be at hazard, incidentally, from sparks thrown from the locomotive chimneys. From contemporary drawings and the sardine-like packing of both second and third class passengers into open trucks it would seem that none of them carried any luggage at all. It could be understood that most of the travel on the Liverpool and Manchester Railway would have been of the day-trip kind, but Ackermann's famous drawing of the interior of Euston, shortly after its opening, shows an equally packed train, on which presumably quite a few of the passengers would be heading for Birmingham. Again, while one would not look to J.M.W. Turner's vividly impressionistic *Rain, Steam and Speed* for accurate historical detail of travel on the Great Western in its first days, a whole string of open thirds, again packed with people, is indicated immediately behind that strange looking locomotive. Reproductions of original drawings, from which more recent copies have been made, show that they were literally open trucks. In his evidence before the Gauge Commissioners in 1845, Seymour Clarke, traffic manager of the Great Western, referred to them as 'common waggons'.

A bad accident in the deep cutting at Sonning in the early hours of Christmas Eve 1841, threw a vivid light upon the way third class passengers were then conveyed. The faster trains were first and second only and, believe it or not, the 'common wagons' were frequently marshalled into *goods trains*. This was revealed in the Sonning Cutting accident. In the dead of night there was a landslide and a large pile of debris spewed out across the down line. At that time there were only two tracks. The engine of the 4.30 am train ran into the obstruction, and stopped abruptly, and the 'common wagons', full of passengers, were crushed between the derailed engine and the heavily loaded goods wagons behind, which, without any brakes could not be stopped. Of the 38 passengers crowded into two trucks, eight were killed and 17 severely injured, in this very reprehensible accident. The Inspecting Officer of the Board of Trade found no fault with the design of the cutting, and considered that the landslip was a natural phenomenon which could have happened regardless; but he had some very strong remarks to make about the way the train was marshalled. It is believed, however, that only the Great Western and the London and South Western Railways made a practice of marshalling open third class wagons into goods trains!

In November 1844 W.E. Gladstone, then President of the Board of Trade, piloted his Regulation of Railways Act through Parliament and this compelled the companies to run at least one train a day on all lines that stopped at all stations, conveyed third class passengers in carriages that had seats, and were protected from the weather, at the fare of one penny per mile. The inclusive speed, including stops, was to be not less than 12 mph. To meet this requirement, the Great Western, on the broad gauge, introduced some quite fearsome closed-in six-wheelers. It seemed as though the responsible authorities said to themselves 'Well, the people are to be sheltered: right, we'll shut them completely in!' These 'boxes', which measured 20 feet by 8 feet inside had ten planks laterally, all except one to take six seated passengers. There were two narrow doors on each side, so that those who wished to reach the more distant seats had to climb amongst already seated passengers. There were four fixed ventilators on each side, and four open spaces, which could be closed by sliding shutters. In such way did our forefathers travel at one penny a mile. What the atmosphere must have been like, inside, on a hot summer's day, staggers the imagination.

Even after larger carriages were introduced there seemed great reluctance to give third class passengers any glimpse of the passing scene. The Great Western put on some rather terrifying iron-bodied thirds in 1848, which had no more than four tiny peep-holes at the top of each of the doors. Though they must have been noisy things they were an improvement in one respect, that the seven doors on either side did give ready access to the transverse seats, and that one did not have to climb over other passengers to reach the more remote accommodation. These carriages were 26 feet 8 inches long inside, and seated 78 people, including the brake man, who sat among the passengers to operate the hand brake when the driver gave the necessary code on the engine whistle. A single oil lamp in the middle was all the illumination that the passengers got at night time.

A very early Great Western four-wheeler, which had only two doors on each side and plain benches inside (British Railways).

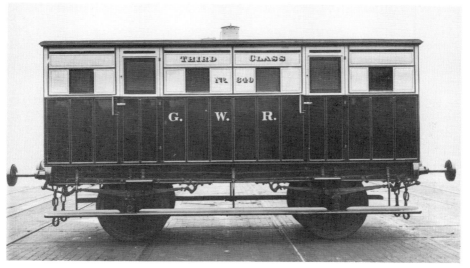

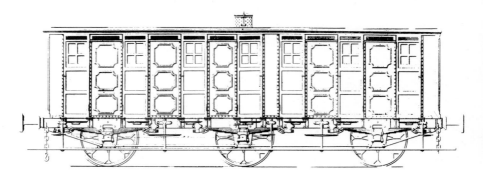

Above *An iron-bodied third class six-wheeler: Great Western Railway* (British Railways). **Opposite page top** *An iron-bodied open-sided 'third', as used on the Vale of Neath Railway* (British Railways). **Centre** *A curious broad-gauge tri-composite four-wheeler, with one compartment each for first, second and third class and one for luggage* (British Railways). **Bottom** *Broad-gauge first class four-wheeler, with papier-maché panels* (British Railways).

The spartan, and latterly decrepit nature of the third class carriages on many of the smaller English railways prevailed for many years. Writing of the South Eastern Railway, in the early 1870s, the famous historian and wit E.L. Ahrons commented: 'Most of the carriages were undersized and four wheeled, nevertheless the wheel bases appeared to be many and various; but there were a number of six-wheelers to be seen, probably constructed when all the possible dimensions of four-wheeled coaches had been exhausted. The styles of windows included Gothic, Norman, and Early English in great variety, intermingled with Elizabethan and Tudor samples. The prevailing window was, however, shaped on the old stage-coach pattern, the middle window of each compartment being rectangular and the side ones shaped at the bottom with rounded curves on the partition sides'.

Of the interior Ahrons wrote: 'This took the form of a cheerless bare rectangular box with hard wooden seats and "half-way" partitions separating the compartments. The partitions were so low that when the passenger sat down with his back to one of them, his head nearly collided with the back hair and best hat of the female in the next compartment'.

Believe it or not, carriages answering precisely to the above description were still in regular use in large numbers in the early 1920s on the suburban services of the Great Eastern Railway, and on the North London. When visiting the Lakeside and Haverthwaite Railway in Easter 1980, my hosts there showed me one of the latter that they had rescued from oblivion, but were astonished to hear that I had actually travelled in them—admittedly quite a few years ago. The antiquarian with an interest in old railway rolling stock could spend many fascinating days, nay months!, searching round country districts where many coach, and covered-wagon bodies, minus wheels, may be unearthed doing duties as garden sheds, hen roosts, or even improvised dwellings. Having discovered the item, to decide upon its ancestry can pose many a problem, even to an experienced connoisseur of old carriages.

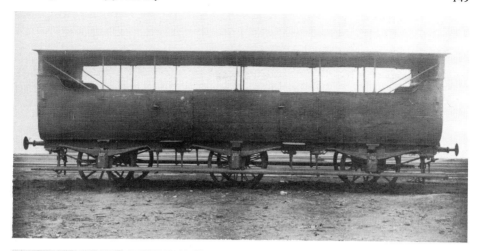

Passing on to the rather better types of old carriage stock, in due course the properly sealed off compartment (as in the original 'firsts') was adopted for all classes, although the accommodation inside was rather cramped. A four-wheeler on the London and North Western, with a body 30 feet long had five compartments, each seating ten. The windows were quite generous, and extended to the full width between the timber uprights. With few exceptions, like the unspeakable 'armour-plated' broad-gauge six-wheelers of the Great Western, all British coaching stock down to the turn of the century was constructed almost entirely in timber, even when much larger and commodious eight-wheelers began to appear. Many beautiful and painstaking restorations of old carriages have been undertaken, not only by the National Railway Museum, but also by the increasing number of private railways now operating in Great Britain. Carriage restoration is no light task, because on many vehicles that have been rescued the timberwork has been found to be sadly dilapidated, and requiring almost complete *replacement*, rather than just 'a wash and brush up'.

Below *The Midland led the way in providing comfort for third class passengers: a neat six-wheeler seating 50 passengers* (British Railways). **Bottom** *A Midland travelling post office van in 1879, with lighting in day time from a clerestory roof.*

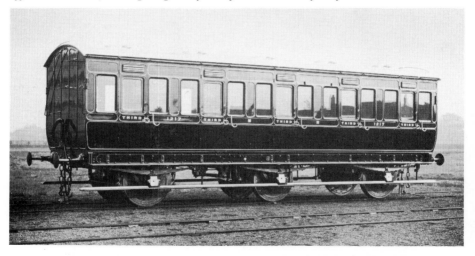

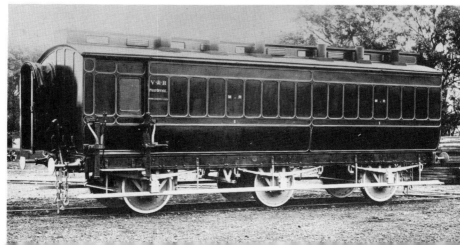

The climax of six-wheeler elegance: a replica of the 'Flying Scotsman' of 1888, restored for the Golden Jubilee pageantry of 1938, and drawn by the Stirling 8 foot 4-2-2 engine No 1, near Hitchin.

What became the usual form of construction, with massive timber uprights, and panelling between, led to some very handsome little carriages that on most British railways were beautifully finished outside. On lines like the Midland and the London and North Western great care was taken with the painting, in many cases to include the company's coat of arms, applied by transfer. The panelled form of construction lent itself ideally to much decorative lining out, though the interiors of the 'thirds' were still inclined to be plain, and rather cheerless. It was the complaint of many passengers that it would have been appreciated more if the railways had paid more attention to the insides rather than the outsides of their coaching stock. One of the most distinctive, if not the most handsome of mid-Victorian carriage styles was that of the Highland Railway, in which the vertical timbers were allowed to protrude strongly on the outside, whereas most carriage styles of the period contrived to bring the panelling nearly, if not entirely, flush with the structural uprights. It is curious that the Highland, which had one of the most elaborate engine painting styles anywhere in the United Kingdom, should, for most of the 19th century, have painted their carriages in a dull all-over green.

A feature of the coaches used on branch lines in the Victorian era is a reminder of the rather primitive arrangements that prevailed at many country stations, and in the older sections of larger stations too. Arising, no doubt, from the need for stage coaches to be boarded from road level, the early railway platforms were very low and, as carriage design progressed, continuous footboards were provided at a level corresponding with the wheel centres, about two feet above rail level. Some companies put a second continuous board at the level of the main frame of the coach, whereas others contented themselves with putting a single footstep below each door. Beside each door a stout rail was fitted, for passengers climbing the steps from a low level platform to grasp. Even on main line express trains running at 60 mph or more, the six-wheeler remained the most usual type almost down to the turn of the century. The record running of the East Coast competitor in the very exciting Race to the North in 1895, when speeds of well over 80 mph were attained on some sections, was composed entirely of six-wheeled coaches! By that time, of course, the accommodation, even for third class passengers, had become vastly better, and a Great Northern six-wheeler, 36 feet long, had only five compartments, and seated a total of 50 passengers.

Despite the introduction of a few American-built Pullman cars, of great size, and with the open saloon type of seating, the compartment type, with its relative privacy, remained a firm favourite in Great Britain. Its incorporation, in a composite sleeping carriage for use on the Kings Cross-Aberdeen route, is remarkable. In anticipation of the opening of the Forth Bridge, and a considerably accelerated service by the East Coast Route, the Great Nothern built some new sleeping cars, at their Doncaster works in 1889, which included separate first and second class compartments in addition to the central sleeping berth section. The use of these remarkable six-wheeled vehicles on the racing 8 pm from Kings Cross in August 1895 has been immortalised by a letter from a celebrated railway enthusiast of the day Norman D. Macdonald, of Edinburgh, to *The Railway Gazette* some 40 years later. To appreciate the force of that letter of reminiscence one must study the plan view of the coach. He wrote:

'The last week of the Race was nearly the death of a group of famous and infamous folk i.e. the Rev. W.J. Scott, Sir William Acworth, C. Rous-Marten, Percy Caldecott, W.M. Gilbert and myself. It fell on this-wise. My East Coast friends (N.E.R., N.B.R., and G.N.R.) always put on a ''sleeper'' for my party when any new spurt effort came to the birth. Till I got the N.E.R. to build the

The first-ever British sleeping car, built by the North British Railway in 1873. Similar cars to this were used on the Aberdeen racing train of 1895 (Nineteenth Century Railway Carriages).

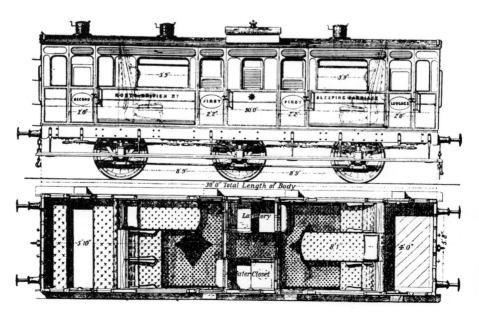

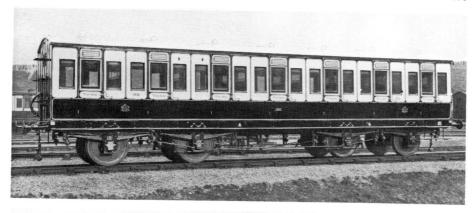

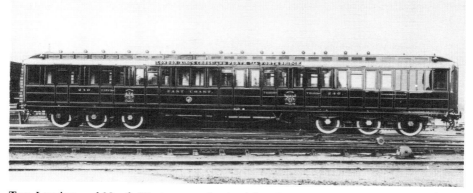

Top *London and North Western non-bogie eight-wheeled 'third' seating 70 passengers, built in 1886. The inner axles were rigid with the hornplates fixed to the sole-bars, but the outer axles were mounted on frames having curved guide blocks to allow a certain amount of lateral movement in a circular arc* (British Railways). **Above** *Turn of the century elegance: a Great Northern-built 12-wheeled composite for the Anglo-Scottish traffic, with the elaborate destination board on the roof, indicating that the train would cross the Forth Bridge* (British Railways).

first transverse-berthed "sleeper" these were made up of cabins of two beds placed longitudinally, entered from a passage across the car.

'At Portobello (Edinburgh) there then was a very bad S-curve with our usual half-hearted British elevation, ending in a high bridge above a wide road.

'At Inveresk Rous-Marten, with his four split watches (one in each hand and one in each trousers pocket) called, "82 m.p.h.". I said, "If these two big Worsdells don't slack off we will be thrown through the windows, even if we stay on the rails at the Portobello S." I quickly got the six into the cross passage, where we jammed our legs and arms against the walls, myself at one window and Rous-Marten at the other. Just before the curves he called "$81\frac{1}{2}$", and I yelled, "Look out!" as we struck it. The whole of them were thrown to me, and we collapsed, as does a Rugby maul, and in the next second we were hurled up again and on to the top of C.R.-M. In his dry Dutch way he was heard to say, "We would have made bonnie raspberry jam in that Duddington road!" ' The

A picnic saloon.

incident was featured in the BBC television presentation, *Race to the North*, in 1978.

The long persisting British predilection for six-wheeled coaches was evident when the London and North Western Railway built their first dining cars, in 1888. They were marshalled in pairs, each one no more than 34 feet long, and connected to each other by a vestibule; but there was no communication at either of the outer ends of the pair with the rest of the train. The accommodation was very lavish. One saloon seated no more than 14 passengers, only one on each side of the central gangway. The second carriage included the kitchen, 'butler's pantry', and a dining and smoking saloon for eight passengers. The windows beside the tables were fixed, but ample ventilation was provided from a clerestory in the roof that ran the entire length of the carriage. This form of ventilation became a standard feature of LNWR dining cars for many years subsequently. The use of the clerestory in the cars of 1888 was the first departure on the part of Wolverton carriage works from the almost flat-roofed type of construction. One would imagine, however, that a six-wheeled dining car did not provide very steady riding, because they were soon altered to have bogies.

A beautiful drawing of the pair of them, both on bogies, is lettered in Old English characters, even down to indicating such functional items as the vestibule between the two cars, and the 'Gents'! There would not have been any stencils for producing that decorative lettering, and the time taken by this draughtsman doing it all by hand must have been considerable. The border round the drawing has elaborate corner ornamentation, rather suggesting that it had been made for presentation before the Board, as well as for use in the shops. That drawing is as much a period piece as the carriages themselves. With the transition from six-wheelers to bogie stock, however, the story of coach evolution passes from the medieval to the modern age.

Chapter 13

Locomotives—quaint and historic

There has surely never been a machine the history of which has been more completely researched, documented and photographed than the British railway steam locomotive. The seeker in technical libraries will find minutely detailed accounts of the complete locomotive stocks of most of the old individual railway companies, some accompanied by a wealth of technical expertise, others at least profusely illustrated, if not entirely by photographs, then certainly by expertly researched line drawings. Faced with such a profusion of evidence one might well wonder what is left, in the field of locomotives, for the railway archaeologist. As one who has contributed several volumes to the literature of the subject of locomotive history I might well find a first approach to the subject rather daunting. What is there fresh to be said? But then, of course, there is the basic approach to the fundamentals of archaeology itself: 'the science which deduces a knowledge of past times from the study of their existing remains'. What was it like to drive and fire a locomotive in the early days of railways? This is a thing that one can scarcely begin to imagine from all the documentation that now exists; and the work of contemporary artists, exquisite though it is in other respects, usually depicts the enginemen in white trousers, and nonchalant postures on their locomotives!

One must, however, put first things first, and before there could be any question of driving locomotives they had to be made. At the time of writing this chapter, in April 1980, intense advance publicity is being showered upon the forthcoming re-enactment of the Rainhill trials, and the pageantry that is to go with it. The construction of reliable working replicas of the competing locomotives of 1829 has been a fascinating exercise; but while it has given Michael Satow and his friends many a headache they have had, in many cases, the advantage of modern production methods, and it is hoped that these replicas will prove more reliable than some of the original competitors. It was when the famous firm of Robert Stephenson and Company received an order from the great American automobile tycoon, Henry Ford, to build for his museum in Chicago a *duplicate* of the original *Rocket*, in the 1930s, that the problems became so formidable. Because Ford did not merely want something that *looked* like the original; every part had to be made in exactly the same way as the original. He did not actually specify that the method of manufacture was to be the same; but the end result had to be. How Stephenson's achieved this, admittedly with the aid of a blank cheque from Mr Ford (!), is a matter of history. No such facility was available to Michael Satow and his friends, in

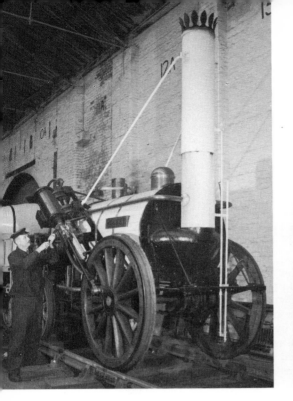

preparation for 'Rocket-150'. But it is interesting to recall some of the production methods that were all that was available to the men of 150 years ago.

A major problem that faced the early locomotive builders was that of producing satisfactory wheels. This may seem surprising seeing that the wheel had been the basic element of transport for centuries earlier; but never previously had wheels been called upon to carry such loads, and to be the means of the transmission of power. While George Stephenson was engineer, and the driving force behind the building of the Stockton and Darlington Railway, he went to Liverpool to survey and build the Liverpool and Manchester Railway. Timothy Hackworth was left at Shildon to carry the heat and burden of the day on the first ever public railway—and a very severe burden it was, at times. From the experience he gained in running the railway Hackworth evolved a freight locomotive of his own, the *Royal George*, that included his own very distinctive type of wheel.

In 1827, when the engine was built, there were no lathes in the Shildon Works large enough to turn up the rims of the wheels when they were fitted upon the axles. So, they were made up from a series of cast iron parts. The centre part, or boss, was machined true, and the outer sections trued by the centre and made tight by a series of wooden plugs and iron wedges. This picturesque type of wheel, which was used on the majority of locomotives Hackworth built for the Stockton and Darlington Railway, can be seen on the preserved goods engine *Derwent* that used to be on a pedestal in Bank Top station, Darlington, but which is now at the North Road Museum. The preserved Stephenson locomotive, *Locomotion No 1* of the Stockton and Darlington Railway, in its familiar and much photographed form, also had 'plug' wheels, though these had been fitted by Hackworth, at some time after the locomotive had featured in the historic opening of the railway in September 1825. The working replica of this engine, built by Michael Satow for the 150th anniversary, in 1975, also had the plug type of wheel.

In building his ill-fated *Sans Pareil* for the Rainhill competition, Hackworth is reported by R. Weatherburn as having included one of the first ever complete wrought iron wheels with 11 round spokes. But an original drawing in the Science Museum at South Kensington shows a very different design, which Robert Young, in his famous biography, *Timothy Hackworth and the Locomotive* describes as having hardwood spokes, and 12 of them, while the engine actually preserved in the museum has cast iron spoked wheels. Such are some of the vagaries that beset those who try to trace early locomotive history. From an engraving in *The Arcana of Science and Art*, published in 1830, it would seem that the *Sans Pareil* did its trial running at Rainhill with wheels, as shown in the South Kensington drawing. What is curious, however, is that Hackworth, otherwise so wedded to the plug type of wheel, should not have used it in his vital competing locomotive. It is well known, however, that he was struggling against excessive weight, and he may have resorted to the wooden-spoked wheel for this reason.

The method developed for making all-wrought iron wheels towards the end of the 1830s by John Dewrance, engineer of the Liverpool and Manchester Railway, provides a vivid picture of the labour and intricacy involved. His wheel had 14 spokes, each forged separately and in itself representing a portion of the boss and a portion of the rim. After the 14 pieces had been placed in position, a strong hoop including two out-jutting lugs encircled the whole. The clamping bolt was then tightened to the utmost, and any badly fitting places wedged up with sheet iron. Then the whole assembly was lifted and placed on what was then called an island hearth, and slowly heated until the wedges became in a

Above far left *The replica of Stephenson's famous* Rocket, *1980—and an engineer makes some final adjustments* (The British Tourist Authority).

Above left *Steaming trials of the replica* Rocket, *August 1979* (Crown Copyright).

Right *The original* Sans Pareil, *in the Science Museum, South Kensington* (The Science Museum).

Left *The* Invicta, *built for the Canterbury and Whitstable Railway in 1830, now restored. This photograph is believed to have been taken when the engine was prepared for display at the Paris Exhibition of 1900* (Crown Copyright).

Below right *What* Hardwicke *was like when first built in 1873. Engine No 1518,* Countess, *illustrated here, was one of 96 2-4-0s of John Ramsbottom's 'Newton' class, first introduced in 1866. Hardwicke was one of the last ten built, and was renewed to its present form in April 1892.*

welding state. The clamping bolt was again tightened to the utmost, forcing the wedges of the spokes together until they were completely united, welding 28 faces at one time. There were several different shapes of spoke and central wedge, in order to build up the pear-shaped boss that would eventually provide a base for the crank pin. The washers providing the raised surfaces of the central boss were added as a separate welding operation. There were then none of the modern aids to fabrication by welding. Fusion of the metal was secured entirely by heat and pressure, and the skill of the blacksmith. This was before the day of the steam hammer.

In the *Rocket*, Robert Stephenson's entry for the Rainhill competition, the tubular boiler suggested by Booth was incorporated, and it duly became the prototype of nearly every steam locomotive boiler built subsequently. Hackworth, on the other hand, used his return-flue type of boiler, in which the grate and fire-door was at the same end as the chimney. This meant that in actual running the engine was turned back to front, as it were, with the chimney adjacent to the tender. The driver was accommodated on a wooden shelf, at the opposite end of the boiler. For the Rainhill competition the entrants were required to furnish only the locomotives. The tenders were 'free-issue' by the Liverpool and Manchester Railway, and those for the *Rocket* and the *Sans Pareil* appear to have been identical. Although the latter failed to complete the course at Rainhill, because of the bursting open of one of the cylinders, it was soon repaired and, without further alteration, worked for many years on the Bolton and Leigh Railway, and later as a stationary boiler. It was retired in 1863.

That it was not then scrapped was due to the interest and generosity of Mr John Hick, Member of Parliament for Bolton, who received the ancient engine from John Hargreaves, of the Bolton and Leigh Railway, and presented it to the South Kensington Museum. The name of John Hick will be familiar to students of London and North Western locomotive history because, in 1894, F.W. Webb named the first of a new series of his three cylinder compound express engines after him, and the series became known as the 'John Hick' class. Although short lived by some British locomotive standards, and withdrawn from traffic in 1910, the name *John Hick* was perpetuated on a new 4-4-0 express engine of the celebrated 'George the Fifth' class, built at Crewe in February 1913, and not withdrawn until November 1935. Although the name was well-known among locomotive enthusiasts, few, one would imagine, would have associated it with the man to whom posterity is indebted for the preservation of the original *Sans Pareil* of Rainhill 1829.

Hackworth's later engines, with the return flue type of boiler, put in many years of arduous hard-slogging mineral service on the Stockton and Darlington Railway. They were fitted with tenders at each end to equip them for longer and heavier turns of duty. That at the chimney end, on which the fireman rode, was given up entirely to coal, or coke, while the second one, at the driver's end, had nothing except a huge water barrel. The men were, of course, completely exposed to the weather and, looking at some of those old photographs, I have often felt more than a mere academic twinge of sympathy for the fireman when running chimney first, bending down to stoke with his back to the direction of travel. I, also, used to suffer from lumbago! Though no consideration was given to it at the time it seems extraordinary now that, for many years after Rainhill, not the slightest protection from the weather was given to the driver and fireman, even though speeds of 60 mph and more were being regularly attained, with express passenger trains. It was not until the 1850s that even such a concession as a plain weather board was being made on a few locomotives of 'advanced' design.

Apart from the absolute primitives, like the replicas of the Rainhill competitors, and the Liverpool and Manchester 0-4-2 *Lion*, it is something of an experience to mount the footplates of preserved locomotives like the *Columbine* and the *Coppernob*. The former had a very long active career on the London and North Western Railway and, in her later days as an engineering department unit, hauling nothing heavier than a single inspection saloon, and often having to stand for long periods out in the back of beyond while her 'owners' were

One of the most famous of preserved locomotives, the first 8-foot bogie single designed by Patrick Stirling, and built at the Doncaster works of the Great Northern Railway in 1870. It is seen here in the original Railway Museum in 1933.

scrutinising certain structures, she was fitted with a cab, for the well-being of the enginemen. As such, and painted in the famous 'blackberry black' of the LNWR she has for many years graced the National Railway Museum at York—albeit looking something of a misfit. But, on a recent visit there, I was delighted to learn that her cab was being removed, and that one will in future be able to stand on her footplate and allow the imagination run to what it was like struggling over Shap on her, and her kind, around 1850.

Cabs apart, however, *Columbine* is a very historic little engine on two other counts. First of these is that she was the very first engine built at Crewe Works, in 1845; but more important is that she is the sole remaining example of Alexander Allan's design of front-end framing, the origin of which lay in an interesting epoch in the development of the steam locomotive. As described in Chapter 3 of this book the link up between the Grand Junction and the Liverpool and Manchester Railway was at Newton Junction; and although Joseph Locke had laid out the former railway for fast running, the connection was on a very sharp curve, and the early Stephenson 2-2-2 locomotives, developed from the *Rocket*, were not flexible enough to take that curve, and failures occurred through broken crank axles. Locke remained engineer-in-chief and, with close liaison between the two railways, arrangements had been made to combine the locomotive depots and repair shops at Edge Hill, Liverpool, not far from the Moorish Arch. There W.B. Buddicom was in charge, duly reporting to Locke. In 1840, activities had developed to such an extent that Buddicom needed an assistant, and a young Scotsman of 31, Alexander Allan by name, was appointed to the job. At the time the trouble with broken crank axles was becoming acute on all the Grand Junction engines which had inside cylinders.

Allan proposed to move the cylinders outside, thereby permitting the use of a

The LNWR Trevithick-Allan 2-2-2 Columbine, *the first locomotive built at Crewe works, February 1845, as first delivered to the York Railway Museum, for preservation in the LNWR 'blackberry' black livery.*

plain, instead of a cranked axle. At that time, however, locomotive frames were made piecemeal, and suffered from many weaknesses; but Allan designed his new engines, of which *Columbine* was the first, so that the inside frames could be made from one continuous plate from end to end of the locomotive. Furthermore, he introduced an outside framing at the front, which carried the supports for the slide bars and, being very strongly braced to the main inside frame, gave additional support to the cylinders. This picturesque form of front-end framing became characteristic of the railways with which Allan was afterwards associated, and it persisted on the Highland Railway on new locomotives built up to the year 1892. Strangely enough, however, although it had saved the day on the Grand Junction, the significance of the design seems to have been rather lost on Allan's Chief, W.B. Buddicom. When Locke built the Paris and Rouen Railway and needed many locomotives, Buddicom resigned his position on the Grand Junction and, in partnership with William Allcard, one of the men who drove the trains on that memorable opening day of the Liverpool and Manchester Railway, in 1830, formed a locomotive manufactory of his own, in France. The firm of Allcard, Buddicom & Co, built many locomotives for service in France, and one of them has been preserved. Curiously enough, however, the Buddicom engines in France, although outwardly looking like Allan's, had the cylinders fixed only to the outside frames, instead of benefiting from the solid and lasting job of being fixed to both inside and outside frames.

Coppernob is another early classic of locomotive history designed in the style postulated by Edward Bury, and still in existence today through one of the most providential near-misses of the night Blitz of 1940-1. Bury was an engine-designer who arose to comparative fame on a strong wave of early railway politics. The Board of the Liverpool and Manchester Railway was by no means unanimous in his approval of George Stephenson as engineer, and indeed a

Furness Railway: the celebrated Bury 0-4-0 No 3 Coppernob, *now in the National Railway Museum at York* (Ian Allan Ltd).

Liverpool member, James Cropper, fought tooth and nail to get rid of him—without success. Then came the London and Birmingham Railway, with Robert Stephenson as engineer, and Cropper's brother, Edward, fought a similarly vigorous campaign against him in the south. He was successful to the extent of blocking any aspirations of the Stephensons for supplying any locomotives and by securing the astonishing appointment, as locomotive superintendent, of a man who was already a manufacturer in a considerable way. Edward Bury was a man strongly imbued with every commercial instinct and, from being the tool by which the Stephensons were excluded from the supply of any locomotives to the London and Birmingham Railway, he so contrived it that for many years he was the *only* supplier! His locomotives were certainly soundly engineered and well constructed, even if they were not very large or powerful; but, while the many he supplied to the London and Birmingham Railway were scrapped as soon as they became obsolete, it is fortunate that a thoroughly typical example of this phase of locomotive development remains in the Furness Railway No 3, nicknamed *Coppernob*.

It was one of a pair built by the firm of Bury, Curtis and Kennedy in 1846. As there was no through rail communication to the Furness district at that time the two Bury 0-4-0s, Nos 3 and 4, were shipped from Liverpool to Piel Pier, which was then the southern extremity of the line. Both engines far outlived their predecessors of the same type on the LNWR and it was indeed not until 1900 that No 4 was withdrawn from service, No 3 was not retired until 1907. They were both of characteristic Bury design, with bar frames, and the high raised copper firebox which gave rise to the nickname. When the time came for No 3 to be taken out of service she was enthroned on a pedestal at Barrow Central station—not out in the open, but in a sumptuous glass case. There she remained until that night in 1941 when a heavy aerial attack was made on Barrow. The large all-over roof of the station was destroyed, and the glass of her case was shattered by bomb blast. But apart from a few superficial contusions the old engine was undamaged, and was afterwards removed to the comparative safety of the inside of Horwich Works. Now fully restored, it is an object of perennial interest in the sanctuary of the National Railway Museum at York. *Coppernob*, and the other engines of the Bury type on the Furness Railway, never had cabs added, and standing beside her today it is worth pondering a moment upon what it was like to go out from the footplate to the front-end, when running, as the enginemen of early days were frequently called upon to do!

Before leaving the Furness Railway mention must be made again of the engine which might one day provide the incentive for an archaeological 'dig' up at Lindal Moor. It was a goods engine of the then-standard Sharp, Stewart 0-6-0 type, of which there were eventually 53 at work on the line. They were by far the most numerous of all the Furness locomotives and represented, in the 1880s, nearly half the total stock of the company. The first nine of them were supplied in 1866, and the last eight, to the same design, not until 1881. They were sturdy little things, very handsomely styled and, although used almost exclusively on freight, were always kept in immaculate condition in the splendid livery of iron-ore red. The particular engine beneath which the subsidence of the line took place, on October 22 1892, was No 115, one of the very last batch, and then no more than 11 years old. Although the cavity appeared no more than gradually, and the driver and fireman were able to jump clear, there was no saving the engine. What kind of condition her remains are in now, after nearly 90 years, is a matter for conjecture; but it must be remembered that she went down with a

Furness Railway 0-6-0 goods engine of Sharp, Stewart design. It was No 115 of this class that fell into the subsidence at Lindal Moor in 1892, and is still there, about 200 feet below ground (Real Photographs Co Ltd).

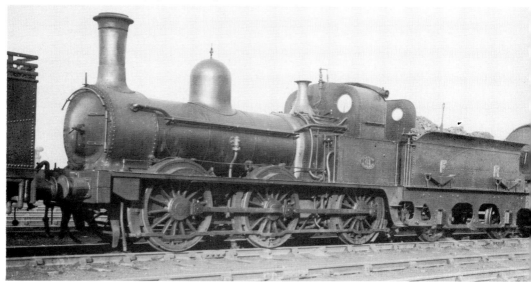

A replica of the broad-gauge 2-2-2 North Star *purchased from Robert Stephenson & Co by the Great Western Railway in 1838, which was scrapped in 1906. The replica was built at Swindon in 1935 to take part in the centenary celebrations of the GWR that year* (British Railways).

full boiler, and her firebox charged for steam production in ordinary freight working. A search for her today has some intriguing possibilities!

George Jackson Churchward, of the GWR is today revered as the prime architect of 20th century locomotive practice at Swindon, of which so many examples have been preserved. That they have a relatively limited sphere of operation in these days of frequent steam specials is due to the Great Western Railway having a somewhat generous loading gauge, as a legacy from the broad gauge of Brunel, and from later engine designers having built locomotives a little wider to take full advantage of it. In the archaeological sense, however, Churchward can be set down as the iconoclast who destroyed two priceless relics of broad gauge days, the locomotives *North Star* and *Lord of the Isles* which, until 1906, had been preserved at Swindon Works. The reason given at the time was that the old engines were occupying space that was required for modern production—the same argument, on a very much larger scale that nearly led to the destruction of the models of early interlocking frames in the Westinghouse Works at Chippenham in 1940. In the March 1906 issue of *The Locomotive Magazine* there appeared the laconic statement: 'Our readers will learn with regret that the two historic broad gauge veterans *North Star* and *Lord of the Isles* have recently been scrapped'. And that was that!

The irony of it was that when the time came for the centenary of the Great Western Railway to be celebrated in 1935 the company had built a replica of the *North Star,* not, it is true, in the form she had been in 1906 but as originally supplied by Robert Stephenson & Co, in 1837. This replica, for which space was found in Swindon Works, is now in the Railway Museum at Swindon. If the stories can be believed, however, nemesis struck G.J. Churchward himself in

1924, three years after he had retired. Then, his successor rebuilt his largest engine *The Great Bear* in so drastic a manner as to amount to virtually scrapping it. It was generally understood that Churchward was very upset about this, even though the engine, whatever its historic function, had always been something of a 'white elephant' as a workaday traffic machine.

But what of the broad gauge engines Churchward himself scrapped in 1906? The *North Star* did not look much like the original engine, having received a later type of boiler, and undergone some alteration to the wheelbase; but the demise of the *Lord of the Isles* was an absolute tragedy. It was built at Swindon in 1850, as a standard engine of the 'Iron Duke' class of 4-2-2s, but did not immediately go into traffic. It was displayed in the Great Exhibition of 1851, in

Below *A scene in the engine house at Swindon, showing one of Daniel Gooch's 2-2-2s, developed from the North Star design.* **Bottom** *Gooch's masterpiece: a broad-gauge 4-2-2 of the 'Lord of the Isles' class, the* Sultan, *as originally built in 1847. It was rebuilt, with cab and a new boiler, in 1876, and was still in main line express service when the broad gauge was finally abolished in 1892* (British Railways).

Above *A broad-gauge express of the Great Western, hauled by the 4-2-2 engine* Timour, *leaving Teignmouth in 1891. Compare to the two later views on the dust jacket.* **Below** *A collection of potential museum pieces in the shadow of historic Whitby Abbey. The Whitby branch of the North Eastern Railway was a happy hunting ground for seekers after ancient locomotives, around the turn of the century.*

Hyde Park, London, and began regular service in 1852. The design, which was developed from the *Great Western* of 1846, was Daniel Gooch's masterpiece, and the *Lord of the Isles* put in 32 years of continuous service, with the same boiler, by which time the engine had run 790,000 miles. Originally, in the fashion of the day, it had no cab, but one was afterwards fitted. This was the only departure from the state of the engine when built. On being taken out of traffic the engine was preserved at Swindon, and duly became something of an exhibition piece. It was displayed at the Edinburgh Exhibition in 1890; it went to Chicago, in 1893, and afterwards to Earls Court. What a sensation it would have made in the pageant of 'Rocket 150', in 1980. In the spirit of enterprise that dominated the London Midland Region on that occasion the laying in of a short length of mixed gauge track to accommodate the engine would have been the least of their problems.

Nowadays one often hears of railway enthusiasts lamenting that they were born too late—too late to see in actuality and photograph locomotives and other items now known to us only in drawings and photographs. But in some respects what are often called 'the good old days' were not so good after all. With the keen overlooking that now prevails over all railway activity the intention at Swindon to scrap the *North Star* and the *Lord of the Isles* would have gone around like the Fiery Cross, and questions would have been asked as to what the h--l Churchward thought he was doing! News of the impending scrapping would have raised a storm almost equal to that of the Doric Arch at Euston. Even if the GWR had not been dissuaded from their intentions, funds would quickly have been raised to purchase at least one of the locomotives, and to preserve it privately. But one feels that with a man of Churchward's resolve it would have been another case of Charles Stewart and the trees in Haydon Square. Long before the protesters had got fairly into their stride the two engines would have been cut up.

Chapter 14

A concluding miscellany—humour, ephemera and memorabilia

In the preceeding chapters I have been concerned with the hardware of past railways, and the human side of things has so far come into the picture no more than incidentally, from aspects of carriage design and the rigours of early locomotive working. But people were, after all, the sole reason for running passenger trains. Nigh on 50 years ago a London newspaper; short of copy in the 'silly season', sent out a roving reporter to try and glean something of the human drama that lay behind railway travellers; to seek out 'the laughter and tears' that lay behind every journey. As was to be expected his probing enquiries on various long distance express trains met with an impenetrable façade of stony silence, if not hostility, from most of those interrogated. Quite undaunted, this questing journalist next tried the train crews, seeking sidelights on their regular passengers. After some initial reticence the dining car men, between meals, came up with some remarkable stories, which duly got into print. Some of these were so far-fetched that Authority began to have suspicions, whence it was discovered that on one route the dining car crews had developed a game of 'ragging the reporter', with keen competition between different crews as to who could sell him the tallest story!

From its inception, in 1897, *The Railway Magazine* included articles of fiction as well as fact. Some of these are very amusing to read today, though no doubt they were not originally intended to be so; and for a time also, cartoons were a feature of this magazine. These are now of some historical significance, as portraying some of the trends and incidents of travel 80 years ago. There was truth, as well as jest in Sir William Gilbert's droll lines in *The Mikado*, wherein the Emperor is outlining his plans to make 'the punishment fit the crime', and he includes this one: 'The idiot who in railway carriages scribbles on window panes, We only suffer to ride on a buffer in Parliamentary trains'.

Riding on the buffers, not necessarily on parliamentary trains, was a relatively frequent way of fare dodging in the 19th century, and *The Railway Magazine* in its series of cartoons 'Types of Railway Passengers' had one entitled 'The idiotic one', duly engaged in changing the lettering above the seats to suit his own puerile sense of humour. Moreover the vandals of today would seem to have little to add to the activities of their forerunners of 80 to 100 years ago, to judge from another cartoon showing how some people spent their time while travelling!

One of the most unusual and gently subtle pieces of railway advertising was featured over ten months in *The Railway Magazine* during 1911. How it came about, I have no idea. Under the serial title of 'The Epistles of Peggy' there were published, each month from January to October, letters from a bright young thing from London who, with her father, was making an extended tour of Scotland, but—and this was the salient point—entirely over the metals of the North British Railway. The 'epistles' were chattily written, very readable, but contained not a shread of true railway interest other than of the attractive places visited. Some of the illustrations were reproductions of photographs; others however looked like discretely introduced railway posters, but without a hint of the North British. The dedicated 'Railwayac'—contemporary name for the 'gricers' of today—would probably have regarded those two page 'epistles' as an utter waste of space, that ought to have been confined to the advertisement pages; but I must admit to finding them a very pleasant 'period piece'.

In Victorian times the then-comparative novelty of railways, and the dramatic nature of some phases in their operation, proved a great attraction to the producers of melodramatic theatrical pieces. Great ingenuity was often shown in moving trains about on the stage, to provide collisions or other startling effects; and although the railway 'properties' were often of the crudest and most amateurish kind, as seen by professional railwaymen, they certainly contrived to grip audiences, both here and in the USA. A contributor to *The Railway Magazine* for December 1899 wrote: 'Nothing is more incomprehensible to the seasoned railwayman than the sustained popularity on theatrical boards of the sensational railway effect. Whether it be due to the excessive demand on his powers of make-believe or to the preposterous nature of the surroundings, the

Below left *The Epistles of Peggy* (The Railway Magazine). **Below right** *A theatrical poster showing the railway tragedy in* The Seven Sisters (The Railway Magazine Illustrated, 1899).

fact remains that for him the stage, with all its marvellous powers of illusion, is incapable of affording anything but a travesty of the varying incidents which go to make up the sum total of his workaday life. Wanting, however, in *vraisemblance*, as may be these effects, they have still a remarkable hold on the public. Some idea of the value set in professional circles upon a more or less ingenious railway "sensation" can be gained when it is said that the costliest and most protracted theatrical lawsuit ever tried in America was a tussle between two managers for the possession of a blood-curdling contrivance of the sort'.

Some of the posters advertising these productions are good for a laugh, as indicating the woeful lack of railway knowledge by theatrical producers, and their poster artists: a fight to the death between hero and villain, in the middle of the 'four-foot', the heroine lying unconscious across one of the rails, and a night express bearing down upon them, unable to stop. In the poster advertising *The Red Signal*, the track layout and the position of the signals make a somewhat diverting study, quite apart from the obvious imminence of a collision. Posters apart, the way locomotives and carriages were made to disintegrate on the actual stage, when the collisions took place, would reduce a modern audience to helpless laughter.

It is fascinating to attempt to trace how the attitude of what is now popularly called the 'media' changed towards railways, once they became an established institution in the country. In the pioneer days no praise was lavish enough to bestow upon the achievements of the engineers. Great artists like Bourne produced magnificent portfolios of drawings showing the great works under construction, and the first trains running. These drawings were made on the sites, and portrayed the scenes with most satisfying accuracy; but once railways had become an acknowledged and commonplace mode of travel they became the butt of any penny-a-liner journalist in need of some quick copy, and over the years an incredible amount of rubbish got into print. The more responsible writers, when they ventured into the railway scene, were not entirely free from blame. It is remarkable today, when other activities such as banking, the motor car industry and air travel are most exhaustively researched to provide highly authoritative backgrounds to best-selling novels, that when railways do get involved the result is either sketchy or inaccurate.

Popular literature devoted exclusively to railways can be said to date from the founding of *The Railway Magazine* in July 1897 but, prior to that, general references in other works can be both interesting and amusing. One of the oldest of such books, in my possession, is a ninth edition of a large and relatively expensive book, *The Scottish Tourist*, the first edition of which came out early enough for Sir Walter Scott to be sent a complimentary copy. The ninth edition is dated 1849, but although it contains full and accurate references to the railways that had then been built, and new plans of the City of Edinburgh showing the railway routes, there is no suggestion that railways should be used in any of the tours proposed, and the final trip, from Edinburgh to London is made by sea! There are references to the station mileages on the lines from Glasgow to Greenock and to Ayr, but in the many exquisite engravings with which the book is illustrated the suggestion of the presence of railways, where they then existed, is carefully excluded, notably in a panorama of the centre of Edinburgh.

It was far otherwise in a handsome little work of 1848, *The New Illustrated*

Hand-book to Folkestone, published and printed by the owner of a library in the town, which includes, a sub-heading to the main title, 'A Description of the South Eastern Railway' and, so far as the Foord Viaduct is concerned, the text becomes positively lyrical: 'Lightness and loftiness are the prevailing characteristics of this notable work, the piers being of exceedingly slender proportions—not more than six feet in breadth, or one fifth that of the arches, notwithstanding their prodigious height, in comparison with those of a bridge of the usual kind. One fact may convey a notion of the wonderful lightness, in connection with extraordinary compactness and stability of construction, which the engineer (Mr. William Cubitt), has achieved in the structure of this bridge, and which we believe to be without parallel—the pressure of the entire structure is not more than 1200 lbs. on the square foot'. The text also contains the most comprehensive and vivid description of the demolition of the Round Down Cliff, to make way for the line between the Abbots Cliff and the Shakespeare Cliff Tunnels. (See Appendix 2.)

So far as contemporary descriptions are concerned, there are none perhaps so remarkable as those contained in a work of 1838, entitled *The Iron Road Book*. The London and Birmingham, and the Grand Junction Railways had barely been completed, and through railway communication between London, Liverpool and Manchester thereby established, before the London publisher, A.H. Baily & Co, commissioned Francis Coghlan, an authoritative writer of guide books, to produce a *Railway Companion*; and he did it in so remarkably comprehensive way as to form a prototype for much 20th century railway

The text of The New Illustrated Hand-Book to Folkestone *is embellished by this charming engraving of the Foord viaduct.*

The Viaduct, Folkestone,

from Cross Hill

publicity. One cannot resist comparing a section of a route diagram from Coghlan's book of 1838 and the LMS *Track of the Royal Scot* published in 1938. Nevertheless it was the Great Western which had blazed the more modern trail in the early 1920s, with its *Through the Window* paperback, describing the route from Paddington to Penzance; and the LNER countered the LMS publicity of the 1930s with *On Either Side*, describing the east coast main line in a similar way.

Reverting to 1848, however, even while the great Britannia tubular bridge over the Menai Strait was still under construction, an enterprising publisher of the name of Thomas Catherall of Chester, published a *Railway Companion* to the Chester and Holyhead Railway, to which was added a tourist guide to Dublin and its environs. It is, however, very evident that these early travel books on railways were not calculated to appeal to the huddled, unprotected masses in the third-class 'wagons'; and while the authors became very enthusiastic over some of the larger civil engineering works, the railway itself (its equipment and operation) is scarcely mentioned. Coghlan gives an excellent running commentary upon the history and tourist attractions of the towns villages and hamlets along the line, straying as far afield as Stratford-on-Avon on the way north.

One of the earliest books to be devoted exclusively to the business of railways, finance, management, operation and comparisons of the British network with those of other countries was Sir Cusask P. Roney's 500-page tome of 1868. His book is entitled *Rambles on Railways*; and the modern reader might feel that at times he is rambling a little! But as a contemporary work it must rank as a classic. It includes an account of a ride on the footplate of an express engine from Euston to Stafford; a commentary upon the running sore of arguments between the Post Office and the railways over charges of conveyance of mail, and a description of Crewe Works, with a eulogy on the person of John Ramsbottom:

'At the head of the mighty establishments at Crewe—establishments in which, including men and materials, there is a weekly expenditure of about £20,000—over a million a year—is one man who, if he had been in Egypt, with works not a quarter the size and not half so ably carried out, would have been at least a Bey, more probably a Pacha, in Austria a Count of the Holy Empire; in any other country in the world, except England, with crosses and decorations, the ribbons of which would easily make a charming bonnet of existing dimensions. But in England the earnest, persevering, never-tiring JOHN RAMSBOTTOM is John Ramsbottom—no more. It is true that he has European and Transatlantic reputation, and that he is Fellow and Honorary Fellow of innumerable societies, thus abnegating in his person the latter half of the aphorism that says:- "Worth makes the man, the want of it the fellow".

'For without the worth he never would have been the fellow. Probably had Mr. Ramsbottom been a Member of Parliament, he might have hereditary honours by this time. But ere long there will be fresh agitation for distribution of seats, notwithstanding the anger of the Quarterly Review of October, 1867, at the "Conservative Surrender". Then will be the time for Crewe to put forward its claims to have its bone, its sinew, its muscle, its manly vigour, and

Opposite *Compare the route from* The Track of the Royal Scot *booklet* **(top)** *with the route from Coghlan's* The Iron Road Book **(bottom)**.

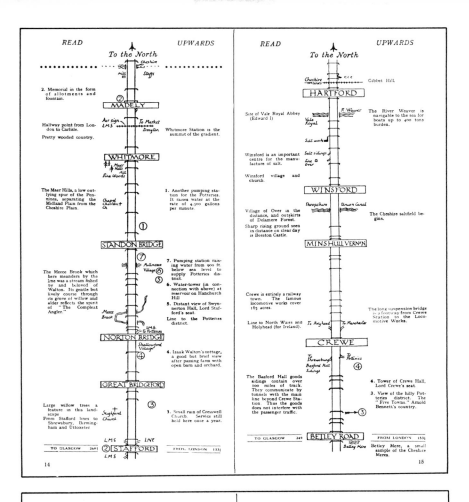

READ *UPWARDS*

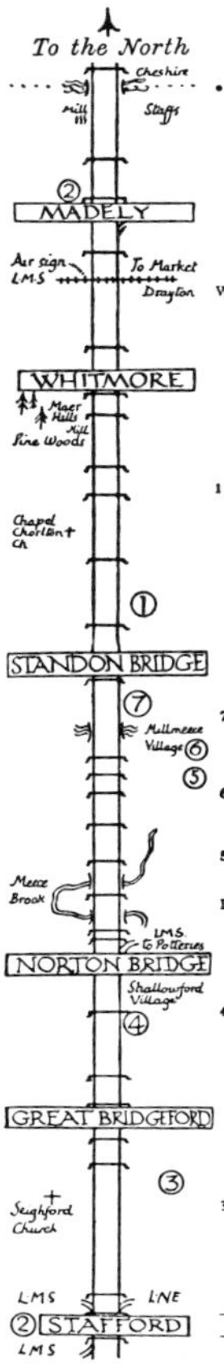
To the North
Cheshire
Mill
Staffs
MADELY
Air sign
L.M.S
To Market Drayton
WHITMORE
Maer Hills
Mill
Pine Woods
Chapel Chorlton Ch
STANDON BRIDGE
Millmeece Village
Meece Brook
L.M.S. to Potteries
NORTON BRIDGE
Shallowford Village
GREAT BRIDGEFORD
Seighford Church
LMS
LNE
STAFFORD
LMS

2. Memorial in the form of allotments and fountain.

Halfway point from London to Carlisle.

Pretty wooded country.

Whitmore Station is the summit of the gradient.

The Maer Hills, a low outlying spur of the Pennines, separating the Midland Plain from the Cheshire Plain.

1. Another pumping station for the Potteries. It raises water at the rate of 4,500 gallons per minute.

7. Pumping station raising water from 900 ft. below sea level to supply Potteries district.

6. Water-tower (in connection with above) at reservoir on Hanchurch Hill

5. Distant view of Swynnerton Hall, Lord Stafford's seat.

Line to the Potteries district.

The Meece Brook which here meanders by the line was a stream fished by and beloved of Walton. Its gentle but lively course through its grove of willow and alder reflects the spirit of "The Compleat Angler."

4. Izaak Walton's cottage, a good but brief view after passing farm with open barn and orchard.

Large willow trees a feature in this landscape

From Stafford lines to Shrewsbury, Birmingham and Uttoxeter

3. Small ruin of Cresswell Church. Service still held here once a year.

TO GLASGOW $268\frac{1}{4}$ | FROM LONDON $133\frac{1}{2}$

READ *UPWARDS*

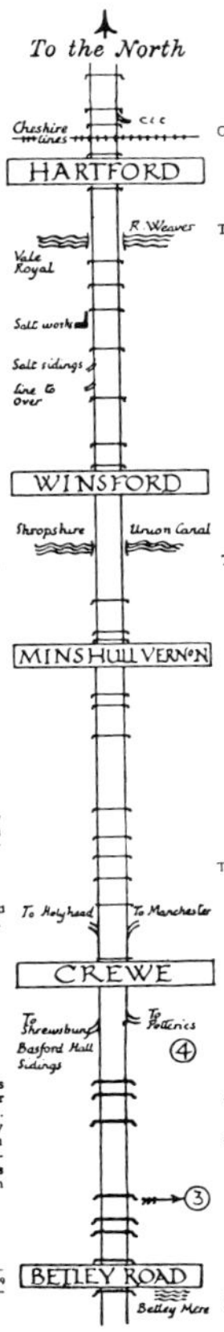
To the North
Cheshire lines
C.L.C
HARTFORD
R. Weaver
Vale Royal
Salt works
Salt sidings
Line to Over
WINSFORD
Shropshire
Union Canal
MINSHULL VERNON
To Holyhead
To Manchester
CREWE
To Shrewsbury
To Potteries
Basford Hall Sidings
BETLEY ROAD
Betley Mere

Gibbet Hill.

Site of Vale Royal Abbey (Edward I)

The River Weaver is navigable to the sea for boats up to 400 tons burden.

Winsford is an important centre for the manufacture of salt.

Winsford village and church.

Village of Over in the distance, and outskirts of Delamere Forest.

Sharp rising ground seen in distance on clear day is Beeston Castle.

The Cheshire saltfield begins.

Crewe is entirely a railway town. The famous locomotive works cover 165 acres.

The long suspension bridge is a footway from Crewe Station to the Locomotive Works.

Line to North Wales and Holyhead (for Ireland).

The Basford Hall goods sidings contain over 100 miles of track. They communicate by tunnels with the main line beyond Crewe Station. Thus the goods does not interfere with the passenger traffic.

4. Tower of Crewe Hall, Lord Crewe's seat.

3. View of the hilly Potteries district. The "Five Towns." Arnold Bennett's country.

TO GLASGOW 249 | FROM LONDON $153\frac{1}{4}$

Betley Mere, a small sample of the Cheshire Meres.

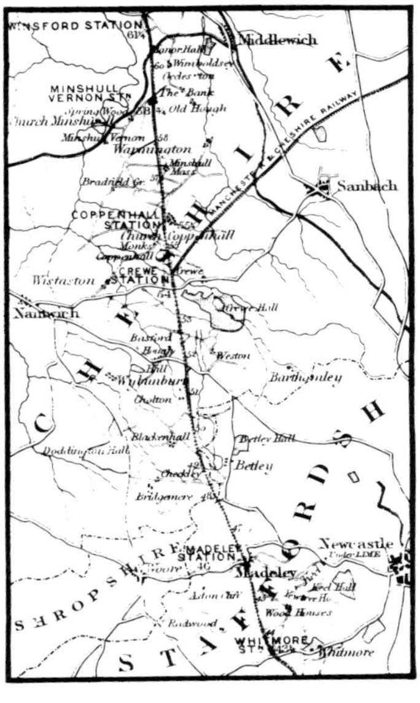
WINSFORD STATION
Middlewich
MINSHULL VERNON STN
Sanbach
MANCHESTER & CHESHIRE RAILWAY
COPPENHALL STATION
CREWE STATION
Nantwich
Betley
Bartholmley
Madeley
MADELEY STATION
Newcastle
WHITMORE STN
Whitmore
SHROPSHIRE
STAFFORDSHIRE

Standon, a parish in the hundred of Pinehill, containing about five hundred inhabitants. The living is a rectory in the archdeaconry of Stafford, rated in the king's books at £6 18. 4. The river Sow bounds the parish on the south. Ten poor children are taught to read for £6 per year, the interest of bequests by two ladies named Tagg and Plant. The church, with the richly-wooded country around it, forms a pleasing object.	$38\frac{3}{4}$	*Standon Cottage*, belonging to Mr. Lunt.
	Emban.	*Hatton Mill.*—Here may be perceived
	$40\frac{1}{4}$	*Trentham Park*, in the midst of which stands the Hall, a very ancient building, inhabited by the Duke of Sutherland. The river Trent runs near to it, to which the park probably owes its name. The house may just be discerned among the trees in the distance. We now begin to approach the third principal station
	Emban.	
	$41\frac{1}{4}$	
	Slight Excav.	
	$42\frac{1}{2}$	
Maerwood.	Deep Excav.	Another *Swinnerton Park*—there being two of that name in the neighbourhood—brings us to

WHITMORE STATION.

$43\frac{1}{4}$ Miles.

ARRIVAL of the TRAINS from BIRMINGHAM.		ARRIVAL of TRAINS from LIVERPOOL & MANCHESTER.	
First Train	55m. past 7	First Train	10m. past 9
Second Train	59m. past 10	Second Train	35m. past 11
Third Train	25m. past 1	Third Train	10m. past 2
Fourth Train	25m. past 4	Fourth Train	10m. past 5
Fifth Train	59m. past 6	Fifth Train	35m. past 7
Sixth Srain	55m. past 8	Sixth Train	10m. past 9

Coaches daily to Shrewsbury, through Market Drayton, at 9 o'clock A.M. A coach daily to Drayton, at 5 o'clock P.M. A coach through Newcastle to the Potteries daily. An omnibus daily to Drayton. The Pottery Company's omnibus daily to Newcastle and Potteries, at 9 o'clock and 11 A.M., and 5 and 7 o'clock P.M.

Left.		Right.
To *Market Drayton*. Near this spot is one of the highest points of the line, the road inclining towards Liverpool one way, and towards Birmingham the other. On a con-	Bridge 44 Excav.	To the Potteries and *Newcastle-under-Lyme*, a borough and market town, and a place of some antiquity. The name was taken from a castle built here by Edmund, Earl of Lan-

Titanic power represented. Who more worthy to represent it than the present semi-sovereign prince who sways, with nearly omnipotent power, $157\frac{1}{2}$ miles from the supreme and sovereign authority at Euston? Add Barrow-in-Furness, and then "King Iron" would make his thunder heard in St. Stephens!'

A period piece of immense interest was a practical manual, *Locomotive Engine Driving* by Michael Reynolds, a locomotive inspector on the Brighton Railway, which was first published in 1877. The author begins his preface thus: 'I am anxious to extend and improve the social condition of locomotive drivers by placing within their reach a standard test of capacity that will be unaffected by local or temporary prejudices, fancies, fashions, or accidental connections.

'It appears to me that our enginemen of today will be to those of the next century what Puffing Billy in 1825 is to the *Monarch of Speed* in 1877 . . .'.

The 'hard' cover of this fascinating book has, as its centrepiece, a beautiful representation, entirely blocked in gold, of one of John Ramsbottom's celebrated 'Lady of the Lake' class 2-2-2 express locomotives, built at Crewe, the *Pandora*, although in the text prominence is naturally given to the Stroudley 2-2-2 engines of the 'Grosvenor' class, of the London, Brighton and South Coast Railway.

Mention, a little earlier, of Barrow-in-Furness, my home town for 14 eventful years, leads me to the publicity and advertising activities of the Furness Railway, for its size, surely, one of the most enterprising of all the old railway companies. As a small boy I had become attracted to the picture postcard displays on railway stations. The South Eastern and Chatham had a series of locomotives, carriages and stations which I used to see on the bookstalls at Reading and Folkestone, but those of the Furness were something completely apart. There were superb black-and-white portraits of locomotives and other items of rolling stock, but it was the series of dramatically beautiful scenes in the Lake District that fairly caught the eye. It was not until many years later that I learned of the origin of those cards. In the early years of the 20th century, a famous publishing house, with which, more recently, I have had very happy

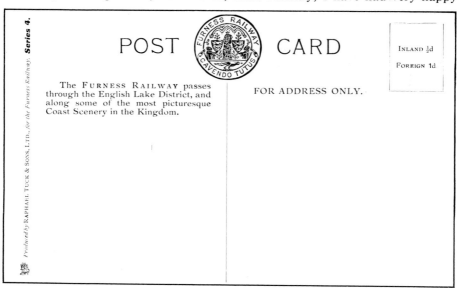

Below left *The reverse side of the Furness Railway postcard.*

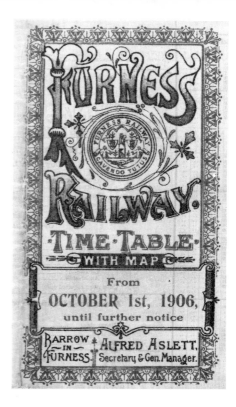

Right *The Furness Railway pocket time-table of 1906.*

associations, was issuing a series of superbly illustrated books, entirely in colour from the work of celebrated artists of the day. This series included one entitled 'The English Lakes' with reproductions of no less than 70 paintings by a noted Lakeland artist, A. Heaton Cooper. The Furness Railway swooped upon this and arranged to reproduce these lovely pictures as penny postcards, with their own imprint and company crest on the back, and the name of the nearest station to the scene depicted on the front.

From Furness Railway literature of those far-off days before the fateful year, 1914, one reads wistfully in some of the old pamphlets of the incredibly cheap day excursion tickets that were available on the line. There was a train leaving Furness Abbey at 2 pm which connected with the afternoon steamer up Windermere lake, reaching Ambleside at 4.5 pm; it returned at 4.20 and got us back to Furness Abbey two hours later, the whole trip costing just half-a-crown! And I have no doubt that my sister and I travelled for half that modest fare. One can, indeed, linger and wonder, verily in disbelief, at the cheap fare facilities that were then offered to passengers, in comparison to the fares that we now have to pay, until one is brought to mother earth with a resounding crash. Turning over one of those Furness Railway postcards one reads that the inland postage was one half penny. If this was multiplied upwards to the 10p it now costs to send a postcard within the United Kingdom, and multiplying that seemingly bargain price rail excursion fare by a proportionate amount it would cost more than £3 to go from Barrow to Ambleside and back—not so cheap after all!

The Great Western issued a series of seven pocket books at one penny each, or the complete set, in a cardboard case for sixpence. These were no summary tables, but a complete symposium of every passenger train on the line. That for

The front and back cover of the GWR pocket timetable of 1904.

the Birmingham and Worcester District, of which I have a copy for the year 1904, had a page size of $4\frac{3}{8}$ inches by $2\frac{7}{8}$ inches, but no fewer than 96 pages. It included not only times of all the trains but the standard cab fares to no less than 60 destinations in and around the City of Worcester, for another 30 from Great Malvern, and in Birmingham separate fares for four-wheeled and two-wheeled cabs, each drawn by one horse. But perhaps the most remarkable item to a railway enthusiast is that on the main line to and from London there was only one train in each direction that had a restaurant car. The fastest train between Birmingham and Paddington then took 2 hours 20 minutes, non-stop, while the much advertised dining car express, leaving Birmingham at 5.45 pm, took exactly 3 hours with stops at Leamington, Banbury, Oxford and Reading.

That first decade of the 20th century was certainly the time in Great Britain when railways were still the pre-eminent means of long distance travel and, except for one or two 'dark areas', they were still considered as a gilt-edged security for the investor. Dividends on ordinary shares varied from around three per cent, in the case of the steady earners, up to five to seven for the 'big six', so far as the stock market was concerned. These were the Brighton, the Great Western, the North Western, the South Western, the Midland, and the North Eastern, around the turn of the century. There was fierce competition for traffic in many areas and the contemporary advertising of the companies, one against each other, makes a diverting study nowadays. The London and South Western, for example, had a pictorial map prominently headed 'In the path of the sun for health and pleasure', and extending from London to mid-Cornwall. The resorts served by the LSWR were shown basking in sunshine, and those of the Great

Western in unrelieved gloom. The GWR had, of course, got away to a flying start at the beginning of this century with its 'Cornish Riviera' gimmick—if I may call it so. The genius in the advertising department who discovered that a mirror image of the map of Italy looked remarkably like Cornwall would probably have been surprised at the way the 'Riviera' concept caught on. The GWR followed it with the famous 'Lucky Dogs' poster, showing three very happy canine passengers sitting on Paddington station with labels on their collars for Penzance, Torquay and Newquay.

Some of the most amusing features of early railway advertising lie as much in the costumes of the travellers as in the alluring prospects laid before the prospective patrons. The West Coast companies, London and North Western and Caledonian, had some very eye-catching posters for what they called the 'white train'. While the joint stock was always painted in the LNWR colours— white upper panels and deep brown bodies—the Caledonian also had white panels, but very deep purple below the waist line. But those passengers—! One showed a dashingly dressed young thing, with an enormous hat, waving farewell out of a third class carriage, beside a strident caption which read: 'The popular pleasure places of Merrie England, as well as London, are best reached by the West Coast Route'. This was followed by another showing an immaculate 'gent', with a silk hat polished, surely, to match the 'blackberry black' shine of an LNWR express locomotive—third class too!—assuring us that there was no better way to London and the chief commercial cities of England than by the West Coast route.

The Caledonian seemed to take a very elegant view of the sartorial styles of its passengers, not only on the West Coast main line trains. They had a poster advertising all the year round cheap day facilities from Glasgow to the Clyde coast resorts, of which the centrepiece was a picture entitled: 'The setting sun as seen across the silvery sea'. Gazing across at this pleasant scene, which might be vaguely reminiscent of the entrance to the Kyles of Bute, were a lady and gentleman—she in particular!—in costumes more suited to Ascot than the West Highlands. Another delightful glimpse of English holiday dress of the early 1900s is given in some posters advertising the Great Eastern hotel at Harwich, in which children, as well as grown-ups figure prominently. The Great Eastern also hit upon a novel way to encourage golfers to travel to the many excellent courses in East Anglia by issuing attractively produced scoring cards for use on the different links.

Towards the end of that halcyon pre-1914 era the business enterprise of the Great Central Railway knew no bounds, though its ordinary shareholders, who did not receive any dividend at all between 1899 and 1912, cannot have viewed some of its major schemes of capital expenditure with any great enthusiasm. It had a very striking 'map' poster in which its territory was cleverly shown on a human hand, and its main line prominently marked as the 'line of health'. But in 1912 most of its activities were centered upon the Royal opening of Immingham Dock, on which great hopes were based for a profitable trade with Continental Europe across the North Sea. Already passenger steamer services had been established from Grimsby to Esbjerg, Hamburg, Antwerp and Rotterdam, as shown in one very striking poster; but the hopes of Immingham were centred on freight, at a time when the overseas trade of Great Britain was touching Olympian heights. Sadly, however, no great business enterprise was hit more severely by the First World War than that of the Great Central, at

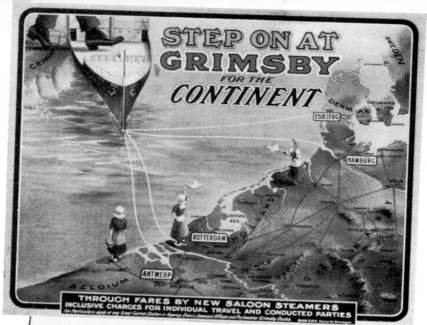

STEP ON AT
GRIMSBY
FOR THE
CONTINENT

ESBJERG

HAMBURG

ROTTERDAM

HOLLAND

ANTWERP

BELGIUM

THROUGH FARES BY NEW SALOON STEAMERS
INCLUSIVE CHARGES FOR INDIVIDUAL TRAVEL AND CONDUCTED PARTIES
For Particulars apply at any Great Central Station or Agency, Town & Liverpool Offices and Dockmaster Grimsby Docks.   SAM FAY, General Manager.

IMMINGHAM Grimsby
THE NEW PORT
FOR THE WORLD'S COMMERCE

ENGLAND'S LATEST PORT
IMMINGHAM
(Grimsby)
DEEP WATER DOCK

VIEW OF COAL HOISTS CAPABLE OF SHIPPING 5,000 TONS PER HOUR.
Accommodation for 11,600 Loaded Wagons, 170 Miles of Sidings
AVAILABLE FOR THE LARGEST SHIPS AT ALL TIDES
DOCK MASTER IMMINGHAM DOCK, GRIMSBY.

Opposite page top *Great Central advertising: Grimsby* (The Railway Magazine).

Opposite page centre and bottom *Great Central advertising: Immingham* (The Railway Magazine).

Right *GNR poster: 'Skegness is so bracing'.*

Immingham; and no more than a startling poster remains to remind us of what was hoped for in 1912 when it was opened by King George V and Queen Mary.

Some railway posters of that decade may be amusing to modern eyes, while others, intended to be funny at the time, now look rather 'corny'; but it was the advertising department of the Great Northern Railway that really 'hit the jackpot' with some really splendid posters which can still be enjoyed today in their original context. It was in 1908 that the once-celebrated, non-stop corridor excursion trains from Kings Cross to Skegness were introduced, first on Good Friday and then at various other dates, for the astonishing return fare of three shillings! But it is the poster advertising the trip that remains a classic: the rotund and rubicund old sailor prancing along the beach like a two-year-old to the caption 'Skegness is *so* bracing'. Another delightful Great Northern poster, advertising the 'bracing east coast air' as the 'Medicine for Children', showed two little toddlers in a bottle, surrounded by crabs, lobsters and other inhabitants of shallow waters, to which were subjoined the resorts Skegness, Sutton-on-Sea, Mablethorpe, Sheringham, Whitby, Scarborough, Cromer and Bridlington, in that order.

The Great Northern advertised for the business man, as well as for the holiday maker, and another eye-catching poster displayed the possibilities of a trip to Edinburgh, with six vignettes showing the major events of the journey there and back. The times make an interesting contrast to what can be done today by the HST service, when one can leave Kings Cross at 08.00, have six hours in Edinburgh, and be back in Kings Cross at 22.02 the same day.

One of the most extraordinary pieces of railway timetable advertising was contained in a poster issued by the London and North Western Railway in 1908:

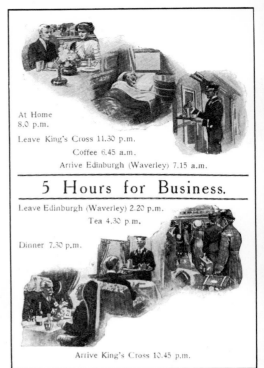

At Home
8.0 p.m.

Leave King's Cross 11.30 p.m.
Coffee 6.45 a.m.
Arrive Edinburgh (Waverley) 7.15 a.m.

5 Hours for Business.

Leave Edinburgh (Waverley) 2.20 p.m.
Tea 4.30 p.m.

Dinner 7.30 p.m.

Arrive King's Cross 10.45 p.m.

Above left *LNWR Euston to the seaside without a stop: 209¼ miles, Euston to Rhyl (British Railways).* **Above right** *GNR businessman's advertisement.* **Below** *LNWR poster—Euston to Japan.*

'Euston & Japan in $22\frac{1}{2}$ days! It was a joint project with the Canadian Pacific, and advertised the 'All British Route via Liverpool, Montreal and Vancouver'. The steamers were, of course, those of the CPR sailing up the St Lawrence direct from Liverpool to Montreal in summer, but in winter landing passengers at Halifax, Nova Scotia, with a railway journey thence to Montreal. The trains and the ships were shown on a very attractive composite poster but, in view of the traditional length and weight of Canadian trains in more recent times, it is interesting to see on this poster that the CPR 4-6-0 is hauling only six large cars, whereas the LNWR 'Precursor' class 4-4-0 has at least nine carriages actually shown on a train that is stretching beyond the limits of the poster! Having arrived in Japanese waters the direct steamer service continued from Yokohama, to Kobe, Nagasaki, Shanghai and Hong Kong. This kind of world-wide advertising was typical of the London and North Western Railway in its most expansive days. There was an old joke in railway circles that averred that when explorers did eventually reach the North Pole they would find there a North Western engine and a brake van waiting for traffic!

*   *   *

The idea of the LNWR at the North Pole is perhaps an appropriate note on which to end this somewhat gossipy final chapter, in which I have ranged round among many topics concerning railways as they were before the summer of 1914. In the examples I have quoted I have nevertheless done no more than touch upon the fringe of the vast field of literature and other documentation that awaits he, or she, who wishes to dive into the archaeology of railways, taking the subject in its very broadest sense. Apart from my own ramblings in this final chapter, each of the preceeding ones could form the subject of a specialist 'dig', which if not so exciting or hazardous as caving, thousands of feet below the surface in the mountains of Northern Spain, or seeking out canoes of the head hunters of the Solomon Islands, could prove invaluable as building up an authentic picture of the travel habits of the British people during the great sociological evolution that began with the opening of the Liverpool and Manchester Railway, 150 years ago. And so far as a real 'dig' goes, there is the ever-present challenge of Furness Railway No 115, somewhere beneath the surface of the line at Lindal Moor!

Appendices

1 The loss and 'recovery' of '115'

The circumstances leading to the loss, recovery, restoration and exhibition, in York railway museum, of the long buried Furness goods engine, No 115, are worth recording while the memory of them remains fresh. The facts are as follows—about 8.30 am on October 22 1892, at Lindal-in-Furness on the main line of the old Furness Railway, an up empty coke train headed by the then-new 0-6-0 D1 class No 115 was put into number 2 up loop in order to allow passage for the morning slow passenger train from Barrow to Carnforth. The empty coke train consisted of 45 high-side dumb-buffer wagons, mainly of private ownership, with two brake vans at the rear. As soon as the train had slowly entered (not backed) into the siding, both guards screwed their brakes down hard; this practice was common at this particular location in view of the slightly falling grade in the up direction. In view of the immediately subsequent happenings the circumstance was fortunate in preventing greater loss of rolling stock.

Number 115 was in the charge of James Anderson with Henry Thompson as fireman. Both men were from Barrow Shed and both fully experienced in the working of this particular train. It should be explained, at this point, that the whole Lindal area was honeycombed with active and worked out haematite mines, that some trouble had already occurred due to minor settlements of the formation (at this point on a high bank some eight tracks wide) and that the up and down main lines were actually laid on longitudinals for half a mile or so with a view to greater distribution of load. The empty train had been standing for about eight minutes when it was passed, at about 25 miles an hour, by the slow passenger train which had just left Lindal station, about half a mile to the west. This train consisted of E1 class 2-4-0 No 57 hauling six 13-ton six-wheelers and a four-wheel brake. James Anderson had been busy oiling up, while his fireman had taken the opportunity of clearing his fire for the scheduled non-stop run to Carnforth. Both men stated that no out-of-the-ordinary circumstances occurred to account for the extraordinary events which transpired immediately subsequent to the passing of the passenger train.

Climbing back to the footplate, Anderson kept his eye on the goods starting signal situated on the north side of the tracks, west of Red Syke Bridge, where the Ulverston-Barrow road crossed the railway. In normal circumstances this signal would be pulled off about four minutes after the passing of the main line train on the latter passing Ulverston west signal box. The first evidence of anything unusual was a steady dipping downward of the forward end of No 115; after about one minute of this, there was a sudden subsidence under the whole engine accompanied by a subterranean rumbling sound as a gaping chasm opened in the formation. Although the tracks did not part, they canted over to the south and thus allowed 115 to fall over sideways and hang at an angle of some 60 degrees, mainly supported by the tender coupling; the latter vehicle, although hard down on the front springs, remained on reasonably solid track and ground.

Anderson and Thompson, at the first sign of trouble, had blown a series of whistle blasts to attract attention and then left the engine. It was now about 8.45 am and the situation was that a long goods train, held at the rear by two brake vans, was supporting a dangling locomotive over a gradually deepening hole. At this stage Anderson became convinced that unless the coupling between the engine and tender was knocked out, the latter, and possibly a number of wagons, would eventually follow 115 into the hole. The decision facing the men was a difficult one, but their action in view of subsequent events was correct. Obtaining a pinch-bar from a nearby wagon repair depot, Anderson and Thompson succeeded in knocking out the tender coupling pin, thus releasing No 115 which immediately slipped down some 30 feet and was partly covered by a fall of earth and ballast from the south side of the subsidence.

About 9.35 a special breakdown train arrived from Barrow, accompanied by senior officers from the locomotive and traffic departments, and the action of Anderson and Thompson in cutting loose No 115 was favourably commented on. After full discussion and investigation it was decided to make no attempt to recover the engine and, in view of the desirability of restoring traffic as quickly as possible, arrangements were made for relays of trains carrying ballast and stone to fill the subsidence. In the meantime passengers were brought by train to the western boundary of the faulty area, walked some two hundred yards and accommodated in trains standing at the eastern brink and proceeding thence to Ulverston and stations to Carnforth. Goods trains were run at much reduced speeds over the suspected portions of the main line.

So much for the facts of the case. It will now be interesting to look into more recent developments. James Anderson was about 40 years old at the time of the accident and was a native of Furness. Among his children was a son, George, at that time a child of ten. About the year 1905, or when he was some 23 years of age, George emigrated to Australia where, by dint of hard work as a civil engineering contractor he amassed a considerable fortune, retiring in 1945 when about 63 years old. Among George's earliest recollections, the account his father gave of the happenings in 1892 remained vivid through the years, and George formed the ambition of some day recovering the engine which his father had lost. Returning to the United Kingdom in 1950 George immediately went to Lindal and himself surveyed the scene of the catastrophe which had occurred 58 years previously.

To cut a long story short George believed that, by a suitable expenditure of money and ingenuity, No 115 could be recovered, and so he approached the Railway Executive with this suggestion. With some hesitation, and after expert assurance that the job could be done without interfering with the present heavy traffic over the bank, permission was given for George Anderson to commence the work under the general supervision of the area civil engineer. Anderson again visited the site, this time in company with railway officials and the engineers of a prominent firm of civil engineering contractors. In the intervening 58 years the relationship of the nearby road and railway had altered to the extent that, whereas the former was then a rural highway some 20 feet in width, it was now a broad tarmac thoroughfare about 80 feet wide skirting the northern foot of the high bank. It was evident that excavation on the main road side of the bank would present great difficulties of accommodation of plant, although disposition of spoil would be facilitated.

On the south side of the railway bank, however, and having access to the main highway through a narrow occupation tunnel extending under the whole width of the bank, there is a narrow lane providing access to agricultural land. It was decided, therefore, to commence excavations on the south side, drive a falling tunnel under the bank until the engine was reached, and use the narrow lane and occupation tunnel for dump traffic in disposing and replacing the excavated spoil. This spoil was to be dumped temporarily in old sunken areas to the north and west of the main road where surface iron ore workings, long since abandoned, had left scars on the land.

The work commenced early in 1951, the location of No 115 being determined by electronic detector devices which pinpointed a mass of metal lying 275 yards west of the present Red Syke bridge and 43 yards north of the two main lines situated on the south side of the formation. The approximate depth below formation level was 200 feet.

The problem presented, therefore, consisted in driving a slanting tunnel from the foot of the south side of the bank for a distance of 500 feet; the bank being 80 feet high and the engine 200 feet below formation level, the downward end of the tunnel would necessarily be 120 feet lower than the mouth, while the grade of the tunnel would thus be determined as 120 in 500 or 24 per cent. This slanting tunnel would not cut into the bank proper but dive under it into the original ground and it was possible that this was honeycombed, to near the surface, by old iron ore workings, the subsidence of one or all of which had accounted for the original engulfment of No 115. It was probable, therefore, that voids would be encountered and certain that heavy timbering must be employed to prevent the tunnel, and possibly the banks above it, from collapsing. A start was made by hand excavation with a square cross section of about 17 feet, timbered all round to 14 feet. As depth was gained, an 18-inch Decauville track was laid upon which small spoil wagons were hauled by winch on to an external timber ramp from which tipping took place into ordinary dump trucks. It was found, as depth was gained, that the soil was reasonably free from rocky inclusions, and work rapidly progressed until, at the end of ten days' digging and timbering, the shaft was within 50 feet of number 115. At this point the main tunnelling was stopped and a four-foot square-timbered header was driven towards the engine. This course of action was taken in order to disturb as little as possible any subterranean cavity still existing after matter was 'dumped' on top of 115 after the cave-in of 1892. This small section header took only two days to complete and finally struck 115 lying on its right-hand side, on what appeared to be firm ground.

The dumped stone, gravel and assorted old sleepers from the 1892 fill formed a fairly compact mass on top of the locomotive. It appeared probable, therefore, that the original subsidence had been very local, that much of the bank material had filled up a hole into the remains of which No 115 had finally fallen and that, with careful handling, no further subsidence need be feared. These facts having been established, the main 14-foot square-timbered tunnel was completed for the remaining distance and excavation round and over the engine was begun in order to form an underground chamber in which No 115 could be righted and prepared for its ascent into the world it so abruptly left nearly 60 years before.

The underground chamber was about 30 feet cube and the most difficult part of its construction was the floor under the old locomotive. The method of procedure was as follows—the two vertical end walls, as heavy timber partitions with concrete footings, were built in adits driven at the front and rear of the engine. A horizontal adit was then driven over the engine with timbering to form a roof; when sufficient clearance was obtained, a sub-roof was erected to form shuttering and the support for reinforcing bars, and a 24-inch thick concrete ceiling poured over the 30 foot section. Half a dozen stout steel ring bolts were grouted into the pour, the rings projecting down from the eventuating ceiling. It is interesting to note that the concrete was not sent down the main tunnel, but poured from track level down a ten-inch oil well pipe sunk in a few hours by a Scottish oil-rig crew operating on a Sunday.

The situation with respect to the floor and two side walls was more complicated and proceeded as follows, remembering that the underground chamber now consisted of two end walls and a roof with an 'impacted' locomotive in the middle. The side wall containing the entrance to the sloping tunnel was first constructed in the adits driven right and left in the prior building of the timber end walls already mentioned. This side wall was 12-inch concrete, reinforced, the pour being sent down the tunnel. A start was then made in clearing away the dirt and gravel fill over the engine and under the new ceiling; as the depth increased the back wall was roughly timbered, held in place by screw struts taking on the new opposite concrete side wall. In this manner the whole contents of the chamber, other than No 115 itself, was removed down to floor level, leaving the old engine lying on its side on a solid dirt floor.

Wire slings were now passed under the locomotive and up to and through the eye bolts previously provided in the ceiling. When adequate support was available a 12 to 18-inch deep further excavation was made under the engine, this was filled with concrete, the pour being passed down the tunnel, and when the new floor was hard, the slings were slacked back to allow No 115 to rest on a solid foundation. The cross struts between the two side walls were now removed, one by one, and the back wall timbering supported by timber gussets taking on the new floor.

No 115 was then jacked over onto its wheels and the accumulation of soil and gravel round the motion and wheels removed. At the same time the side and connecting rods were dismantled, surprisingly little corrosion being found. A standard gauge light section track was now laid down the 14-foot tunnel, a heavy wire cable secured to the front framing of the engine, and the latter jacked round until it faced the tunnel opening. A powerful winch with suitably placed pulleys was then employed to haul No 115 bodily up the tunnel and out into the open air. The reappearance of the old engine was made a social and historic occasion, there being present not only the usual press, movie, and radio reporters but also senior officials of the Railway Executive with the Mayor of Barrow-in-Furness, the chairman of Dalton Urban and Ulverston Rural District

Councils and the Members of Parliament for Barrow and North Lonsdale. (Those who are interested in fuller particulars in this regard are advised to consult the local and national newspapers for the period involved.)

The engine was then slung by shear legs on to a special low truck which was towed by a powerful tractor along the occupation lane and through the fields beyond it, up a special ramp cut in the south side of the railway bank (here considerably lower than at the site of the excavation), into the west portion of Lindal yard. This course was necessary as the occupation tunnel, already mentioned in connection with the passage of the spoil trucks, was too small for the engine to pass. On arrival in Lindal yard the locomotive was placed on a suitable crocodile wagon by two steam cranes and transported to Horwich Shops for complete overhaul and restoration. The spoil was now returned down the tunnel which was itself eventually filled in.

Some interest may be taken in a description of the general condition of No 115 on arrival at Horwich. The bell mouth funnel was bent and rusted through in one or two places. The cover of the steam dome, the brass safety valve cover over the fire box, and the boiler sheetings were all badly dented while the latter were rusted through in a number of places on the side of the engine which had laid uppermost. The Stirling-type cab and side sheets, together with all the foot plating, was in fair condition and even retained sizeable areas of the original Furness red paint. The front buffer beam, being of timber, was rotten but the cab fittings, boiler and fire box and main frames were in excellent shape. The wheels and motion were rusted but not too badly corroded, while the cylinders and axle boxes had suffered but little by their long entombment.

The whole process of repair and reconditioning took about six weeks and, surprisingly, few new parts were required. Although the original intention had been to restore No 115 as an exhibit only, the general condition was found to be sufficiently good to put the old engine in steam and this was accordingly done. The boiler pressure was, however, dropped from its original 120 lbs per square inch to 80 lbs. The original tender had long been scrapped, but an identical substitute was obtained from the Eastern Region of British Railways where a few old time Sharp tenders were still doing duty as tank wagons.

After a few runs in steam in East Lancashire, the engine and tender were towed light to York, where Mr George Anderson was the central figure in a handing over ceremony to the Railway Museum authorities. And there No 115 stands today in all the restored glory of Furness red, polished brass and gleaming steel. Only an explanatory plaque on the rear wall provides evidence of the unique history and circumstances involved, the satisfactory outcome of which should form an enduring monument to Mr Anderson himself and witness to his enthusiasm and ancestral pride.

*   *   *

This account, which was written by Commander G. Taylor of the Royal Canadian Navy, and which is published again here by courtesy of the Stephenson Locomotive Society, had such a ring of authenticity about it that at least one railway enthusiast 'fell for it' to the extent of going to York to see the recovered engine!

2   The demolishing of the Round Down Cliff

On quitting the Folkestone Station, you proceed for a short distance through the Martello excavation, and enter almost immediately the Martello or Folkestone Tunnel, which is 206 yards in length. You then enter on the Warren or Undercliff, about two miles in length, passed by a series of cuttings, in some parts 120 feet in depth, with most beautiful scenery on the left, and occasional peeps of the sea to the right. At the eastern end of this Warren, the line enters the main chalk cliff, and you proceed through Abbot's Cliff Tunnel, 1,895 yards in length, from which you emerge on the perpendicular face of the cliff about 60 feet above the sea at low water. It then passes within a parapet for about a mile in a straight line, supported by a concrete wall of great thickness. This portion of the line is terminated on the west, towards Folkestone, by Abbot's Cliff, and on the east by Shakespeare's Cliff; the hills are separated by a valley which rises gently upwards to their escarpments, and presents towards the sea a frontage of nearly five miles in extent, at an average height of about 350 feet. This front is nearly perpendicular, with here and there projecting masses of chalk, one of which was called the Round Down Cliff. It rose to the height of 375 feet above the level of the sea, and a passage had to be made in a direct line from Abbot's Cliff to Shakespeare's Cliff. To tunnel it was impossible; to dig it down would have taken it is said 200 men two years, and at an expense of at least £15,000. To remove the obstacle, a mass of chalk rock, 300 feet long and 375 feet high, with an average thickness of 70 feet, Mr Cubitt determined to try the effects of gunpowder, by means of galvanism—one of the boldest attempts, probably, that the mind of man ever conceived. The result of this vast undertaking is so graphically described in the columns of a Metropolitan Journal, that we are sure it will be read with interest.

'Dover, January 26th 1843.—This day the long looked for explosion took place on the works now in progress on the South Eastern Railway, at a part called the Round Down Cliff, situate a short distance from the celebrated Shakespeare Cliff. A great deal of anxiety has been manifested by various parties in consequence of the immense quantity of gunpowder used on the occasion, there being no less than ten tons of that destructive article employed. The sole management of this undertaking was vested in the person of General (late Colonel) Pasley, who it will be remembered, effected the removal of the wreck of the Royal George at Spithead last summer. He arrived here on Tuesday evening in company of a number of the most celebrated engineers of the day, and yesterday completed a general survey of the stupendous undertaking. On our arrival at the spot this morning, we found that every preparation had been made, and every caution taken to prevent accidents. Placards were distributed in the town to that effect, and the 19th Regiment, now stationed at Dover, assisted by the Artillery Corps, who through the whole of the proceedings, have rendered every possible service towards the undertaking, kept parties from approaching too near the scene of action.

Having premised thus much as to the locality of Round Down Cliff, I now proceed to describe, as briefly as I can, the means employed to detach from it such an immense mass of solid matter. Three different galleries, and three different shafts connected with them, were constructed in the cliff. The length of the galleries or passages was about 300 feet. At the bottom of each shaft was a chamber, 11 feet long, 5 feet high, and 4 feet 6 inches wide. In each of the eastern and western chambers, 5,500 lbs of gunpowder were placed, and in the centre chamber 7,500 lbs, making in the whole 18,500 lbs. The gunpowder was in bags, placed in boxes. Loose powder was sprinkled over the bags, of which the mouths were opened, and the bursting charges were in the centre of the main charges. The distance of the charges from the face of the cliff, was from 60 to 70 feet. It was calculated that the powder, before it could find a vent, *must* move 100,000 yards of chalk, or 200,000 tons. It was also confidently expected that it *would move* one million tons. The following preparations were made to ignite this enormous quantity of powder:—At the back of the cliff a wooden shed was constructed, in which three electric batteries were erected. Each battery consisted of 18 Daniels' cylinders, and two common batteries of 20 plates each. To these batteries were attached wires, which communicated at the end of the charge by means of a very fine wire of platina, which the electric fluid, as it passed over it, made red-hot, to fire the powder. The wires covered with ropes, were spread upon the grass to the top of the cliff, and then falling over it were carried to the eastern, the centre, and the western chambers. Lieutenant Hutchinson, of the Royal Engineers, had the command of the three batteries, and it was arranged that when he fired the centre, Mr Hodges and Mr Wright should simultaneously fire the eastern and western batteries. The wires were each 1,000 feet in length, and it was ascertained by experiment that the electric fluid will fire powder at a distance of 2,300 feet of wire. After the chambers were filled with powder, the galleries and passages were all *tamped* up, as is usually the case in all blasting operations. Shortly after 10 o'clock the directors of the company, accompanied by Mr Cubitt, the engineer, and several of their friends, proceeded from the Ship Inn, through the new tunnel recently cut through the rock under the battery, which is also a tunnel in the railroad, to the Shakespeare Tunnel, and thence to the foot of the cliff to be blasted down. After inspecting the face of the rock, they proceeded onwards to the Abbot's Cliff Tunnel. This occupied their attention till one o'clock, when they mounted the top of Round Down Cliff, and proceeded to the marquée at the west-end of the cliff provided for their reception. As the wind blew to the east, the greater part of the distinguished visitants took their station by the western marquée, under the notion that their view would not be so much interrupted by the smoke. Among the number were Sir J. Herschell, General Pasley, Colonel Rice Jones, E.R. Rice, Esq, MP; Professors Sedgwick and Airy; the Rev Dr Cope, Principal of Addiscombe, and others. The surrounding hills and downs were covered with groups of persons—some of whom did homage to the might of gunpowder by keeping at a mile's distance from the scene of the explosion. From the loose manner in which they were scattered about, I can scarcely make a guess at their numbers. Two steamers also put out to sea filled with passengers, and took their position at a distance of about half a mile from the cliff. Two o'clock came, and the general excitement became intense. At ten minutes past two Mr Cubitt ordered the signal flag at the director's marquée to be hoisted, and that was followed by the hoisting of all the rest. A quarter of an hour soon passed in deep anxiety. A maroon was thrown over the cliff, and on its explosion with a loud report, all the flags were hauled down. Four more minutes passed away, two more maroons were fired, and all the flags except that on the point to be blasted were again hoisted. The next minute was one of silent, and breathless, and impatient expectation. Not a word was uttered, except by one lady, who, when too late, wished to be at a greater distance. At exactly 26 minutes past two o'clock, a low, faint indistinct, indiscriminable moaning subterranean rumble was heard, and immediately afterwards the bottom of the cliff began to belly out, and then almost simultaneously about 500 feet in breadth of the summit began gradually, but rapidly, to sink; the earth on which the marquée was placed trembling sensibly under the shock. There was no roaring explosion, no bursting out of fire, no violent and crashing splitting of rocks, and comparatively speaking, very little smoke; for a proceeding of mighty and irrepressible force, it had little or nothing of the appearance of force. The rock seemed as if it had exchanged its solid for a fluid nature, for it glided like a stream into the sea, which was at a distance of about 100 yards— perhaps more—from its base, filling up several large pools of water which had been left by the receding tide. As the chalk, which crumbled into fragments, flowed into the sea without splash or noise, it discoloured the water around with a dark, thick, inky-looking fluid; and when the sinking mass had finally reached its resting-place, a dark brown colour was seen on the different parts of it, which had not been carried off the land. I forgot to minute the time occupied by the descent, but I calculate it was about four or five minutes. The first exclamation which burst from every lip, was, "Splendid! beautiful!" the next were isolated cheers, followed up by three times three general cheers from the spectators, and then by one cheer more. These were caught up by the groups on the surrounding downs, and, as I am informed, by the passengers in the steamers. All were excited—all were delighted at the success of the experiment, and congratulation upon congratulation flowed in upon Mr Cubitt for the magnificent manner in which he had carried his project into execution. Thus terminated an experiment which has been completely crowned with success, and by which it is said the company are gainers to the amount of £7,000. The *debris* of the cliff may be seen at the mouth of Shakespeare's Cliff Tunnel.'

*   *   *

This extract was taken from *The New Illustrated Hand-book to Folkestone, and its picturesque neighbourhood, with a description of the South Eastern Railway*, printed and published by H. Stock, Library, High Street, Folkestone, in 1848.

Index